**YSG
DINA
TREF
NEWPORT
DYFED SA42 0XB
TEL: 01348 811294**

YSG
DIN
TRE
NEW
DYF
TEL: 01348 811294

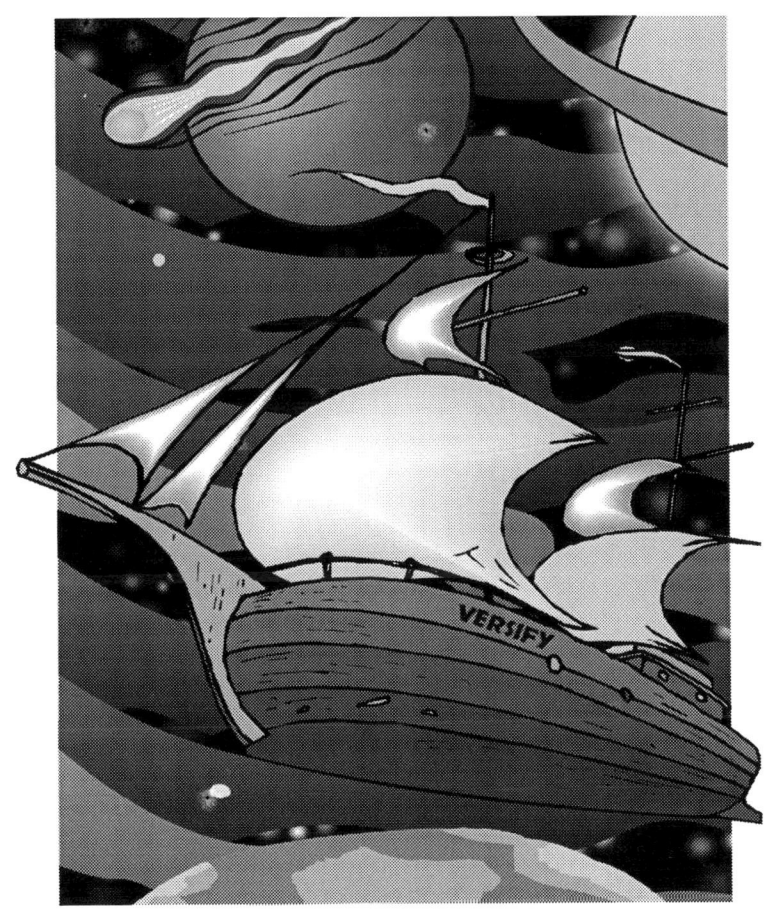

POETIC VOYAGES TO INFINITY AND BEYOND

Edited by Steve Twelvetree

First published in Great Britain in 2002 by
YOUNG WRITERS
Remus House,
Coltsfoot Drive,
Peterborough, PE2 9JX
Telephone (01733) 890066

All Rights Reserved

Copyright Contributors 2001

HB ISBN 0 75433 514 3
SB ISBN 0 75433 515 1

FOREWORD

Young Writers was established in 1991 with the aim to promote creative writing in children, to make reading and writing poetry fun.

This year once again, proved to be a tremendous success with over 88,000 entries received nationwide.

The Poetic Voyages competition has shown us the high standard of work and effort that children are capable of today. It is a reflection of the teaching skills in schools, the enthusiasm and creativity they have injected into their pupils shines clearly within this anthology.

The task of selecting poems was therefore a difficult one but nevertheless, an enjoyable experience. We hope you are as pleased with the final selection in *Poetic Voyages To Infinity And Beyond* as we are.

Contents

Emma Walls	1
Naomi Horobin	1
Matthew Curd	2
Luke McBride	2
Rebekah Lewis	2
Sophie Henderson	3
Sam Antrobus	3
Rebekah Wemyss	4
Alex McWhirter	4
Claire Foley	5
Suzanne Nicholson	5
Larna Wilson	6
Lyndsay Hepplewhite	6
Emily Peters	7
James Curley	7
Iram Ishtiaq	8
Sean Adamson	8
Harry Swinton	9
Rebecca Goodway	9
Emily Dowler	10
Jamie Sharpe	10
Elizabeth McFarlane	10
Zoe Holden	11
Ryan Best	12
Cheryl McGeough	12
Maria Vassiliou	13
Kirsty Thornton	13
James Waters	14
Kimberley Hart	14
Jason Stretton	15
Brodie Jobson	15
Simon Everson	16
Becky Coles	16
Ronald McCaughey	17
Alex Seeley	17
Jade Hutchinson	18

Neil Blincow	18
Hannah Dawson	18
Tayler Fenton & Elinor Lee	19
Gemma Maclellan	19
James Rigby	20
Rachael Weller	20
Shona Johnston	21
Aislinn Faulkner	21
John Henderson	22
Lavinia Copper	22
Chloe Henderson-Gray	23
Martin Hulme	23
Lewis Newton	24
Ben Harpur	24
William Millorit	25
Rory Kelly	25
Yaakov Gluck	26
Stephanie Tett	26
Sadie Hodgson	27
Jonathan Queen	28
Elian Goncalves	28
Krystina Dixon	28
Hannah Barran	29
Paul Southey & Ryan Kalla	30
Jessica Adams	30
Olivia Cantillon	31
Rebecca Kerfoot-Davies	31

Beaver Road Primary School, Manchester
Ayeesha Graham	32

Brilley CE Primary School, Herefordshire
Ellen Baines	32
Daniel Case	33
Jessica Jones	33
Phil Hyde	34
Ben Morris	34
Jake Vaughan	35

Brynhafren CP School, Powys
Louise Bungay	35
Daniel Hughes	36
James Wolstenholme	36
Gemma Botley	37
Matthew Williams	38
Charlie Weaver	38
Jack Lloyd	39
Tom Broom	39
Kimberley Williams	40
Sacha Molin	40
Adam Hilditch	41
Charley Broom	42
Rachel Kelton	42
Millie Andrews	43
Stephen Harrison	44
Robert Bungay	44
Harvey Stringer	45
Sian Santry	45
Alison Hughes	46
Lucy Edwards	46

Carr Manor Primary School, Leeds
Claire Keith	47
Priyen Limbachia	48
Alex Baron	48
Tiffany Hussain	49
Elizabeth Dishman	50
Harshna Karsan	50
Rachel Bailey	51
Thomas Lainchbury	51
Laura Hudson	52
Sophie Dixon	52
Graham Matthews	53
Manveer Batebajwe	54

Clyro Church In Wales Primary School, Powys
Twm Jones	55
Eleanor Pattison	56
Josh Pattison	57
Billy Trigg	58
Bethan Eckley	59
Thomas Griffiths	60
Sophie Green	61

Darkley Primary School, Co Armagh
Conor Murphy	62
Peter McParland	62
Laura Comiskey	63

Denend Primary School, Fife
Jade McConville	64
Craig Chrisp	64
Scott Ormiston	65
Margaret Jamieson	65
Ross Halleron	66
Kim McCathie	66
Richard Wood	66
Nicola Shand	67
Michelle Rankin	68
William Braid	68
Elaine Moyes	69
Kimberley Wilson	69

Dinas CP School, Pembrokeshire
Ed Stockham	70
Tilly Macrae	70
Michael Evans	71
Rachael Evans	71
Tom Parkes	72
Mathew Reading	73
Matthew Holmes	74

Ferguslie Primary School, Renfrewshire
- Fiona McKechnie — 75
- Louise Bain — 76
- Kayleigh McCramigle — 76
- Laura Leitch — 76
- Toni Lauchlan — 77
- Kenny Tarbert — 77

Hartside Primary School, Co Durham
- Jade Birkett — 78
- Danny Parker-Brooks — 78
- Paul Harvey — 79
- Ruth Cranston — 79
- Antony Howcroft — 79
- Josh Craig — 80
- Rebecca Anderson — 80
- Hayley Walton — 80
- Nathan Gilchrist — 81
- Hayley Trotter — 81
- Sarah Clarey — 81
- Anthony Conley — 82
- Charmaine O'Brien — 82
- Laura Hook — 82
- Laura Winter — 83

Kingsway Primary School, Merseyside
- Lesley Seddon — 83
- Nadia Forbes — 84
- Danielle Morgan — 84
- Corinne Upton — 85
- Daniel Sanders — 85
- Zoe Dalton — 86
- Dayle Dunlop — 86
- Michaela Carson — 87
- Samantha Carr — 87

Larbert Village Primary School, Stirlingshire
        Rebecca Fleming   88

Lindridge CE Primary School, Worcestershire
        Rachael Gwilt   88
        Sarah Jones   89
        Lucy Wylde   89
        Tanita Pardoe   90
        Tess Champion   91
        Thomas Jeffrey   92
        David Sherriff   92
        Charlotte Ginger   93
        Michelle Hargreaves   93
        Leigh Hanson   94
        Louise Potter   94
        Joel Brook   94
        Joshua Thompson   95
        Lydia Millichap   95
        Penny Sherriff   96
        William Dayson   96

Merstham CP School, Surrey
        Joanna Webber   97
        Elizabeth Stanger   98
        Karla-Ann Dauncey   98
        Katie Ballard   99
        Nathaniel Harper   100
        Laura Jane Boxall   101
        Alexander Bull   102
        Sarah Neil   103
        Luke Cartwright   103
        Mitchell Stevens   104
        Tim Buttle   104
        Darryl Kirby   105
        James Trumper   105

Montbelle Primary School, Kent
- Sarah Bovey — 106
- Charlotte Read — 106
- Kate Elliott & Rebecca Fay-Read — 107
- Katie Morgan — 108
- Charlotte Barker — 109
- Roseanne Ashley-Lahiff — 110

Oaklands Primary School, West London
- Katie Eastwood — 110
- Michaela Bishop — 111
- Maddie Sturgess — 111
- Melanie Fung — 112
- Abbaas Ali Ramzan — 112

Redburn Primary School, Co Down
- Luke Weatherstone — 113
- Corey Burgess — 113
- Patrick Short — 113

Rhydri Primary School, Caerphilly
- Caitlin Simpson — 114
- Elsa Carpenter — 114
- May Lewis — 115
- Seren Thomas — 116

Rosebank Primary School, Leeds
- Maverick Arabskyj — 117
- Marcus Colquhoun — 117
- Anisah Iqbal — 118
- Sarah Blakeborough — 118
- Stephanie Germaine — 119
- Rosie Connelly — 119
- Fehmina Nawaz — 120

Ryelands Primary School, Hertfordshire
Stephanie Cogger	120
Lois Savage	121
Becky Alford	122
Kerry Matthews	122
Ashton Fendick	123
Michelle Partridge	124
Lee Wilson	124
Emma Johnson & Lauren Irons	125
Zoe Constantinides	126
Natasha Ince	127
Daniel Burns	128
Aaron Moss	128
Dean Cann	129
Louise Dedman	129
Jacey Irons	130
Emma Irons	131
Steven Constantinides	131
Ben Tucker	131
Ben Goodliffe	132

Sadberge CE Primary School, Co Durham
Emma Best	132
Elizabeth Muller	133
Clare Eddy	133
Corrine Best	134
Samuel George Teasdale	134
Robyn Bell	135
Richard Berriman	135
Rachel Bird	136
Rebecca Swindells	136
Matthew Evans	137

St Blane's Primary School, Glasgow
Maureen Shanahan	137
Siobhan Adams	138
Ryan McGinley	138

Jennifer McGuire	139
Michael Thomson	139
Jamie Irvine	140

St Cuthbert's RC Primary School, Co Durham

Maria Kelly	140

St John Vianney RC Primary School, Merseyside

John Jackson	141
Sophie Edgerton	141
Chloë-Anne Topping	142
Mark Smith	142
Rachael Scriven	143
Michael Roughley	143
Clare Curtis	143

St Margaret Mary's Junior School, Merseyside

Michael Maloney	144

St Patrick's RC Primary School, Nottinghamshire

Toby Sewell	144
Karl Patterson	145
Jacob Murphy	146
Daniel Withers	146
Stephanie Sewell	147
Marc Patterson	148
Anjali Phakey	148
Marsha Cotter	149
Stephanie Hargreaves	150

St Stephen Churchtown Primary School, Cornwall

Daniel Brown	150
Lindsey Hodgson	151
Laura Manship	151
Dexter Havenhand	152
Michael Wray	153

Salterforth CP School, Lancashire
	John Knock	153
	Michael Haydock	154
	Michael Worden	155
	Grant Armstrong	156
	Carly Locklan	157

Sir Frank Whittle Primary School, Coventry
	Shaun O'Brien	157
	Claire Kelly	158
	Garion Huggard	158
	Bethany Moore	159
	Nikita Hall	160
	Rebecca Mortimer	160
	Jenna Willis	161
	Catherine Berry	162
	Ellis Brown	162
	Hayley Barnes	163
	Kellie Smith	163
	Natalie Hales	164
	Gary Mead	164
	Scott Garner	165
	Aimee Goodall	165
	Phillip McCluskey	166
	Sarah Thompson	166
	Stephanie Ledbrook	167

Skelmorlie Primary School, Ayrshire
	Ashleigh Lesley Hayter	167
	Ross McKenzie	168
	Neil Goldie	168
	Eilidh Wells	169
	Lisa McMunn	170
	Stephen Kerr	171
	Grant Gallacher	172
	Stacey Little	173

Tenbury CE Primary School, Worcestershire
- Cory Rogers — 174
- Jennifer Gould — 174
- Ruth Forman — 175
- Morgan Wrighton — 176
- Rebecca Jenner — 176

Tenby Junior Community School, Pembrokeshire
- John Blazey — 177

The Cathedral School, Essex
- Thomas Barnes — 177
- Matthew Ruffell — 178
- Chisola Chitambala — 179
- Emma White — 180
- Phillip Blood — 180
- Naomi Hammett — 181
- Elizabeth Stark — 181
- Felicity Clarke — 182
- Emma Hammond — 183
- Luke Richmond — 184
- Alexander Fairbairn — 184
- Brinsley Peersman — 185
- Abigail Connor — 185
- Heidi Booth — 186
- William Haswell — 186
- Bethany Hawkings — 186
- Elizabeth Bell — 187
- Liam Speed — 187
- Kimberley Smith — 188
- David Robinson — 189
- Claire Lewis — 189
- Rosie Orgles — 190
- Patrick Whelpdale — 190
- Daniel Schultz — 191
- Thomas King — 191
- Emily Hunt — 192
- Sian Barnes — 192

James Allen	193
Charlie Savage	193
Samuel Moody	194
Sarah Hardy	195
Angharad Eveleigh	196
Amelia Wright	196
Helen King	197
Grace Readings	197
James Greenwood	198
Hannah Mochrie	199
Abby Wood	199
Sam Booth	200
Angus Macnaghten	200
Maria Creasey	201
Angus James Hogg Forfar	201
Cian Cottee	202
Ben Brunning	202
Peter Hawkings	203
Elizabeth Greenwood	204
Guy Schofield	204
Danielle Pavitt	205
Katerina Panteli	206
Edward De Barr	206
Simon Schofield	206
Tess Mochrie	207
Toby Wells	207

Trent Vale CE(CA) Primary School, Staffordshire

Nathan Dabbs	208
Oliver Hopwood	208
Kayleigh Roberts	208
Melanie Griffiths	209
Joshua Pedley	209
Jake Thomas	210
Rachel Rowley	210
Thomas Day	211
Hannah Lynch	211

Westmont School, Isle Of Wight
- Luke Ferguson — 211
- Joshua Broomhead — 212
- Jonathan Reading — 213

Woodland View Middle School, Norwich
- Georgia Long — 213
- Paul Barker — 214
- Charlotte Lawrence — 214
- Joshua Betts — 215
- Anna Watts — 216
- Emily Dixon — 216
- Vicki Tate — 217
- Alex Hopkins — 217
- Rachel Wright-Carruthers — 218
- Kel Haywood — 218
- Rebecca Saunders — 219
- Victoria Reeve — 219
- Amber Kemp — 220
- Craig Inman — 221
- Natalie Steer — 222
- John Fisher — 222
- Kieron Blundell — 223
- Phillip Fordham — 224
- Luke Clements — 224

Ysgol Gymraeg Ynysgedwyn, Powys
- Elin Mary Williams — 224
- Rebecca Steer — 225
- Catrin Hughes — 226
- Nia Wyn Hopton — 227
- Megan Davis — 228

Ysgol Trap, Carmarthenshire
- Stephen Westlake — 229

The Poems

THESE THINGS I LOVE!

These things I love!
Close your eyes sit on a swing
And listen to the birds singing
The wind whistling around me
The revving of a motorbike
Going full speed
These things I love!

Going to the petrol station
Get the machine going for the big journey
I like the smell of ink on a photocopy sheet
The flowers in the garden
Smell and attract bees
Sore heads must go out
For some fresh air
These things I love!

The shine from the sun
Shining upon me
The white fluffy pillowcase
Reminds me of my bed
The colour of yellow brightens
Up my day
These things I loved.

Emma Walls

MONSTERS

Monster, monster come out to play
Monster, monster you are afraid
Monster, monster lived in the wardrobe
And he never comes out to play.

Naomi Horobin (8)

IN THE TRENCHES

I saw the muddy, dirty trenches,
I saw scraps of rock, hard biscuits on the wet ground,
I saw revolting rats scattered everywhere,
I saw the cold rain pouring down into the filthy trenches,
I saw exhausted soldiers scraping past the rusty barbed wire,
I saw the wounded men shriek in pain,
I saw falling men dying in murky no-man's-land,
I saw injured men being rescued,
I saw blood pour out of my throbbing arm.

Matthew Curd (9)

MY BEST PLACE

My best place is in my garden.
The leaves wafting, the wind whistling,
the grass moving and swaying,
the clouds scudding across the sky.
My best place is in my garden,
because there is a den that nobody knows about.
I like it. It is warm and cosy, it smells of all sorts of things,
like grass and soil. I feel warm and snug under my cover.

Luke McBride (7)

UNDERWATER

Underwater is so quiet, I like it down there a lot.
Fish swim wiggle, waggle.
Up and down dolphins go.
Sharks can never catch their meal.
I like underwater seals.
How much I like the underwater world.

Rebekah Lewis

My Bedroom

I can smell bubble bath in every place that I can find.
The sun will melt when it smells it,
And the clouds will be bubbles when they see it.
I hear birds tweeting everywhere, like my little Game Boy.
Rustling draws opening everywhere like they always do.
Reminding me of a train going along its track.
I can see toys in winter and spring and games rattling everywhere.
Also cupboards opening like cars going along on roads
And dirty travels all over the streets and round the world.
I can feel my cuddly toys cuddling up to me
like a big hairy lion would do.
I can feel the wind blowing me away
Like a twister coming forwards to me, blowing my toys away.

Sophie Henderson (7)

Starry Night

When I go to my warm, comfy bed,
My brown hazel eyes both are lead,
To the steamed up window ledge
There seems to be a dazzling light,
In the enchanted silvery night.
I think to myself, what a beautiful star
But it's miles away, so far, so far,
It's perched right beside the cratered moon.
One day I'll be up there, some day soon,
Jupiter, Venus, Pluto, Mars,
Shame we can't go up there in a solar powered car!
If I go up there I'd go alone,
But I think I'd rather stay at home!

Sam Antrobus (8)

GRANNY IN LEATHER

When I am old
I will not knit
I will not be cloaked up in a rocking chair
I will go fishing!
I'm not going to be lazy
I'll dye my hair purple
And go out to nightclubs!
I'll be wrinkled
But I won't care!
I'll have a good time!
I will get a motorbike
And wear chains
I'll take my cat with me
I'll get it a leather coat
Just like mine!

Rebekh Wemyss (11)

SCHOOL

Teachers telling us off,
quite a few of us are boffs.
It's quite cold on the dusty hall floor,
where there's an old rotten door.
It's cleaned quite well by the caretaker,
who's also a famous candle maker.
All the playground games,
portraits of our fame in frames.
I reckon we get too much homework.
In the staffroom, teachers lurk.

That's our school.

Alex McWhirter (10)

Dark

When the lights go out
And it is dark in my room
I wish the morning
Would come soon.
In the middle of the night
I'm as scared as can be
Because I cannot see
What is all around me.
I see spooky shadows
On my room door
But it's only my mum
On the landing floor.
I hear strange footsteps
Coming up the stairs
But it's only my dad
Coming to say his prayers.

Claire Foley (7)

Hands

Stone-launcher
Clothes-dresser
Nose-picker
Pencil-holder
Trumpet player
Window-cleaner
Ball-catcher
Dog-patter
Foot-tickler
Clothes-washer.

Suzanne Nicholson (7)

NEWCASTLE TOWN

Up, up and away in Newcastle Town
Past the Tyne Bridge
Over the Tyne river
Up, up and away.

It was quite hot
I saw some funny looking people
Some good ones too.

Up, up and away in Newcastle Town
Past the Tyne Bridge
Over the Tyne river
Up, up and away.

Better get home now, it's getting late
Hope I come back soon
So up, up and away.

Larna Wilson (8)

MY CAT

My cat is like a ball of twine
She runs around the house
She is a lovely fluffy thing
She also chases a mouse.
My cat is really a funny thing
She never seems to think,
And another thing that is strange about her
Is she seems to give me a blink.
My cat loves to play around
But when she gets angry she makes that awful sound.

Lyndsay Hepplewhite (11)

SNOW

I woke up early
I don't know why
Put on my dressing gown
And rubbed my eye
I felt excited
My room was bright
I pulled back the curtains
The world was white
Out of the night clothes
And into the day
Into the bathroom
Wake Sis on the way
Swallow my cornflakes
Drink up my tea
Pull on my wellies
And it's outside for me
The air was filled with snowballs
I caught one on my head
But climbed the hill determined
To come down on my sled
I made a giant snowman
Laid snow angels on the ground
Then wandered home for dinner
Where a warm fire could be found.

Emily Peters (9)

THE OLD MAN OF DUNDEE

There was an old man of Dundee,
Who decided to sit on a flea,
He itched and itched until he was bit,
And then he fell on his knees.

James Curley (8)

SPACE

3, 2, 1, blast-off
Through each passage
On my own
Passing Mars
Shaped like a dome.

On my journey
On my way
Passing Jupiter
To Saturn, hooray.

Going through
There I can spot,
Earth like a big colourful dot.

Turning back to Earth
3, 2, 1, land!

Iram Ishtiaq (9)

MY BEDROOM

Last week I moved into my new house
I hate it
My bedroom is very scary
I've got ghosts
I hate them too
They really annoy me with their laughs
Why did it have to be me that has scary ghosts?
So I said to my mum,
'I hate this house!'

Sean Adamson (11)

THE MAGIC BOX

I will put in the box
The light from a sparkling star,
A puff from a cloud in the north
And the spark from an electric eel.

I will put in the box
A rotting tooth of a giant,
A shot from a shotgun in a pheasant shoot,
The smoke from a puffing dragon.

I will put in the box
The smell from a sizzling stir-fry,
A flame from the core of the Earth,
A genius from a computer,
The tail from a bright red fox.

Harry Swinton (9)

THE RIDE OF DEATH

Quick, run for your seat,
Hold on tight,
The ride is about to start,
Now close your eyes,
We're going up,
Up to the sky,
Round the corner,
Now we can fly,
Why did I get on this ride,
Is it not what I thought,
Not one bit,
Stop it at once!

Rebecca Goodway (11)

GRANDAD
(Dedicated to Grandad John Wadley)

My grandad is with me
Wherever I go.
I love him and need him,
So sad to let him go.
I know he is with me
In the air that I breathe,
On the ground I walk.
I will always love my grandad,
Why did he have to go?

Emily Dowler (12)

WHAT IS RED?

Red is the sign of love.
Red is a lipstick as red as a rose.
Red is your heart beating hot.
Red is red jelly.
Red is an apple you eat.
Red is a jumper all cosy and warm.
Red is a fireball floating in the air.
Red is something we all love to share.

Jamie Sharpe (7)

POOR AND RICH

Poor, I am poor, I have nothing to do
and I want money and a bit of honey too.
But no one knows that I want money
and a bit of honey.

Rich, I am rich, I am so glad
and now I will never be sad.
So if you had money would you spend it
on a bit of honey too?

Elizabeth McFarlane (8)

WHAT HAS HAPPENED TO . . . ?

Where is my puppy, Mother?
What has happened to pup?
He's not in his basket
But beside it is his favourite cup.

Where can he be, Mother?
I've looked everywhere
He's not in the garden
Mum, how can you not care?

What are you doing with the phone, Mother?
Are you dialling 999?
Oh, I hope you are
Because I want him, he's mine!

What's that noise, Mother?
It's coming from over here
Can I go and have a look Mother?
I think I'm getting near.

It's a police car Mother
What's that barking sound?
Hooray, hooray, it's my puppy
He's been found.

Zoe Holden (10)

IF I WAS ABLE TO PAINT

The sound of a dragonfly's wings colliding as they hover
                                      over the ground
The taste of Galaxy chocolate melting in my mouth
The smell of nectar in beautiful new bloomed flowers
The touch of a puppy's silky cream fur in a spring breeze.

I would like to paint . . .
The taste of Coca-Cola fizzing in my dried out mouth
The sound of birds singing in the lush green trees
The taste of a cucumber crunching in my watery mouth
The sound of sausages sizzling in the blazing frying pan.

If I was able to paint . . .
The sound of chime bars chiming poetically
The touch of a beehive with bumps running down
The smell of sweet honey freshly picked from the hive
The taste of sweet sugar on your morning cereal.

Ryan Best (10)

MY DAD

I love my dad such a lot,
Even if he's fair or not.
When I see him,
My heart starts pounding
Like a train.
It's always sounding.
He's always hip,
He's always cool,
When I see him he's never cruel.
I love his face,
His cheeky grin,
I love my dad deep within.

Cheryl McGeough (11)

NIGHT POEM

The day disappears once again.
The blue dark dull blanket comes.
The stars, they are like little mountain peaks.
The moon is a big huge rock.
A million times bigger than the Earth.
As round as a saucer.

I climbed in my warm, cosy bed feeling safe and secure.
My toys are my bodyguards.
Under my covers I see a shadow.
I peep out, it's just my little baby brother, afraid of the night.
The thunder and lightning are like instruments playing.
After all the noise
The sun came and I was so glad.
A big, huge ball of fire.
As if the sun had beaten the moon!

Maria Vassiliou (10)

JOHN

You passed away peacefully
I won't forget your laugh, or tasty curry

I saw you walking up the farm
Past the farmhouse, past the barn

I won't see you walk anymore
Because you have passed through Heaven's door

I remember how you played golf on the green
You were the best golfer I'd ever seen!

Kirsty Thornton (10)

MY PARROT

My parrot is very colourful
He's got bright blue wings
I think he is wonderful
He is my favourite thing

I like him more than football
I like him more than sweets
I know he is quite small
He's got little yellow feet

I like to cuddle him up in bed
I fiddle with his wings
I stroke his tummy that is red
I've never heard him sing

My parrot is my best friend
I tell him everything
I drive him round the bend
I love his soft blue wings.

James Waters (9)

GLIMMERING FIREWORKS

Fireworks whistling
through the air
like stars glimmering.
Crackling fireworks zooming
through the air.
Bang!
Bang!
Bang!

Kimberley Hart (9)

WEATHER

Thunder roars
Rain pours
Lightning strikes
Dark nights
Spring showers
Green flowers
Flying kites
Morning bites
Snow drops
Flowers pop
Grey sky
Clouds high
Heavy rain
Water drains
Winds blow
Leaves flow
Snow falls
Make balls
No rain
Causes pain.

Jason Stretton (11)

BRODIE

B rodie is my name.
R obby lives next to me.
O ranges are nice.
D ogs are lovely.
I am a good friend.
E lephants are my favourite animals.

Brodie Jobson (8)

SENSATIONS

The notes like an organ are playing,
Echoes vibrating my ears,
Like the lonely sense of a churchyard,
Joined outside with its friends,
The daisies and buttercups are waiting,
Bluebells bob in the breeze,
Singing their song so sweetly,
Not to be picked to spoil their beauty,
But to grow alone by a single seed,
With no one to disturb them.
Petals and leaves are falling
Like a storm of confetti
Like a blanket covering the ground.

Simon Everson (10)

WIND

I am a gentle breeze
Flying like a calm bird
Swirling and whirling
Is what I do best
I am a powerful force
Pushing when I want my way
I'm not as bad as a hurricane
Down every street and lane
Kicking and pushing in tantrums
Blowing you out of the way
I try not to do any damage
But then I can't help myself and explode
I'm not that bad really.

Becky Coles (10)

FIRST LOVE

You're like the stars that shine in the sky
The flowers that lie.
You're like the sun, moon and sky
Love is what I have for you
And it will grow as I grow
When I see you I'm embraced by love, your love
My dreams would come true if I was with you

L ove wider than a blue sky
O cean deep is my love for you
V aster than the starlit heavens
E ternity my love will last

I'm mesmerised by your love
Your heart is as big as my love for you
I'm under your love spell
You would not break my heart
Golden leaves floating
Your face is blooming like a flower
You stole my heart
I love when the stars shine over your golden hair.

Ronald McCaughey

SPIDERS

S piders are the best
P ictures are the best of spiders
I n poems I like to rhyme about spiders
D rawings I like to do spiders the best
E lephants can be scared of spiders sometimes
R eading about spiders I like
S piders I like lots.

Alex Seeley (9)

DRAGON

Mum, there's a dragon in the garden
I tried to stop him from going into the shed
And he just said, 'I am the dragon of green valley hill
So don't try and feed me a sleeping pill.
I know what you're up to, you're trying to kill me.
I warned you if you give me that pill
You'll be in the dungeons of horror hill.'
So Mum just said, 'I've got a bad head,
I need to lie in my bed.'
Mum won't believe me, Dad won't either,
I'll try to feed him a bone, if that doesn't work,
What shall I do!

Jade Hutchinson

EVACUATION

The train station is where my sad story begins,
Hundreds of scared and confused faces,
I'm standing here, clutching my mum and dad's hands,
With the stench of smoke piping around us,
I taste the tears rolling down my face,
There's the whistle, I have to go,
I hope when I come back, I've still got a home.

Neil Blincow (11)

SOME DAYS

On a good day I would be kind and generous.
Go to school, be good.
Do good work.
Play football, have fun.

On a bad day I would be a pain in the neck.
Drive people up the wall.
Wake up, be grumpy.
Shout and have a fight.

Hannah Dawson (10)

THE WITCH'S SPELL

Double, double, toil and trouble,
Fire burn and cauldron bubble.
A bat's wing with a bee's sting,
Bitter bubbles with bats' troubles.
Cast a spell to make you swell,
Your face will go green like an angry queen.
A slimy slug in your mug,
A bat's tail with an angry snail,
A two-headed dog with two green frogs.
Double, double, toil and trouble,
Fire burn and cauldron bubble.

Tayler Fenton & Elinor Lee (8)

WHY DO YOU STARE AT ME?

I stare at you because you are tiny
I look at you because you have soft fur
I study you because you have a ringed tail
I watch you because you are hyperactive
I see you as an interesting strong tiny animal
And I don't know why you are not in the wild.

Gemma Maclellan (9)

A Voyage

Boats turning on their tops,
Sailors mopping up with mops.

Creaking, wet, mouldy wood,
Be careful Ellen really should.

Sailing boats zoom all around,
Because of no engines, not a sound.

To achieve that career she saved her money,
Eating apples when it was sunny.

She hurt her finger on the way,
She had to stick a needle in it to make it okay.

She slept for thirty minutes a day,
When she woke she found a big iceberg in the way.

She did it and was very brave,
When other people would shout and rave.

James Rigby (9)

What Has Happened To The Dolphin?

What has happened to the dolphin Mother?
What has happened to the dolphin?
I've just gone to visit,
To see if we can go for a swim.
There is a hole leading from the pool Mother
Down towards the sea.
Has it swam away Mother?
Has it now got free?

Rachael Weller (10)

WINTER!

Winter comes as white as white,
and all the days get bright.

In the street the children play,
In the snow all day.

Now the day is done and all the fun
we had today we
will have tomorrow
when we play out in the snow.

Today we went to the park to play
but everything was put away
and all that was left was snow.

Every time I go outside it seems as if we
are in a tide of snow and rain and hail.

Rudolph is coming to our house
but still as quiet as a mouse.

Shona Johnston (11)

SCHOOL IS COOL

School is cool
School is me
School is just like a honey bee
You have to do work but who cares
Because teachers have to run up and down stairs
Clarsach is fun
And so is Mum
But school lunch is so yum, yum, yum!
Do your work
And have fun
At school.

Aislinn Faulkner (9)

LIFT-OFF

The numbers were going down
I had a nervous breakdown
The rocket started
I got butterflies in my stomach.

My head crashed
My brain was spinning
I started to float
It was fantastic!

I got to the moon
I'll be getting home soon
The shooting stars
Just like Mars
Gliding through the air.

John Henderson (11)

THE CAT

The cat lays silently on the bed,
Moonlight shining on his head,
Turning his coat a burning red,
While he dreams the night away.

Mice and voles running by,
Whiskers twitch and stir,
Claws outstretched,
He grabs and plays,
Unseen prey he chases.

Ears twitch,
Sounds awaken the lazy mouser.

Lavinia Copper (10)

LEGS IN THE STREET

Legs in the street
Are fat and thin.
Legs in the street
Are bone and skin.

Legs in the street
Are smooth and knobbly.
Legs in the street
Are old and wobbly.

Legs in the street
Skip and jump.
Legs in the street
Run and bump.

Legs in the street
Walking and jogging.
Legs in the street
Tired and slowing.

Chloe Henderson-Gray

KNIGHT'S ARMOUR

Shining like the stars at night,
Worn in a huge scary fight,
Worn by lords, knights as well,
It could even make them all swell.

Scratched and dented all around,
Worth much more than one pound,
Swords flash and arrows fly,
All in battle, you will die!

Martin Hulme (8)

MY NEW SCHOOL

Car park for the cars
Art room for the painting
Library for us to read in
And a hall for us to sing in
A science room to do
Experiments that we like
Best.

Football pitch for us to run around on
Netball court to play on
Equipment for the young ones
Our playground is just the
Best.

Maths room for maths
English room for English
Our school is the best
You will be
Impressed.

Lewis Newton (9)

A POEM

What is a poem?
A poem can say hello
Say goodbye
Maybe even say a lie.
A poem can sing
A poem can cry
A poem doesn't even have to rhyme.
I like poems in every way,
I just wish I had one
For every day!

Ben Harpur (10)

SPACE BAT

He glided in
Pitch-black
Black as coal
Orange blazing eyes
Like Mars burning
Glaring over the world
Gliding over the horizon
With huge, scaly, black wings
Tail lashing like
An axe being swung
Over and over again
This incredible monster
Swooping down like a
Concorde and as fast
As a super powered jet
Zooming down from
Space in the midnight sky.

William Millorit (9)

FARAWAY TOWN

F　ifty miles away from my house,
A　nd over the houses I pass,
R　oaring and laughing I only heard
A　way with my body.
W　hy have I done this?
A　way and I stop,
Y　okes crowd around me.

T　alk to nobody but myself,
O　n the roadway.
W　here nobody finds me.
N　ever forever.

Rory Kelly (10)

THE WIND

Wind blows the clothes on the washing line,
Wind blows the leaves off the trees,
Kappel blows off,
Peyos in the air,
It's cold and shivery
And I feel very, very cold.

The snow
Build a snowman,
Carrot for his nose,
Icy numb fingers
And snowballs to throw,
I feel that I like this weather.

The spring
When spring comes,
Green leaves appear on the trees,
The birds start chirping loudly
And that is my second best weather.

The summer
When summer comes,
The day is longer,
So we can play together,
Thank you Hashem for giving all these things
And that's the most we can say.

Yaakov Gluck (9)

TWINKLING STARS

Twinkle, twinkle star at night
How you shine so bright,
You make the darkness glow
And you'll be frosty when it snows.

Twinkle, twinkle star at night,
Are you the first star I've seen tonight?
I wish I may, I wish I might
See you next time big and bright.

Stephanie Tett (11)

WHAT HAS HAPPENED TO LA-LO?

What has happened to La-Lo Mother?
What has happened to La?
All I can see is her empty bed
Has she ran away?

Where has La-Lo gone Father?
Where has she gone?
The car is not there
Has she been gone for very long?

Is it her, is it her?
I'm sorry darling, it's not
But Mum, but Mum
We miss her such a lot.

Bro, bro, little bro
La-Lo's cupboard is bare
There's nothing, absolutely nothing
Not even a strand of hair.

Oh look, oh look
I've found her old teddy bear
I'm sorry she has ran away darling
Oh no, I really do care.

Sadie Hodgson (10)

HAPPINESS

Happiness looks like the colour blue
Happiness is like an icky glue
Happiness tastes like a rotten fish
Happiness makes a very fine dish
Happiness smells like growing flowers
Happiness looks like the tallest towers
Happiness sounds like a driving car
Happiness feels like singing in a bar.

Jonathan Queen (10)

THE JUNGLE

I went to the jungle,
I saw some monkeys making a bungle,
I saw a snake baking a cake,
I saw a giraffe having a bath
I saw a crocodile who was snappy
It was changing its very big nappy,
I saw a lion using his iron,
I saw a bear with no hair.

Elian Goncalves (8)

MY SNOW POEM

Snow is falling, snow is settling,
No one's about in this white world.
I'm watching it fall, tumble, swirl, twirl,
Watching it form a carpet of white,
Oh, what a pretty sight.

Crystals are twinkling as the sun comes out,
Icicles are dazzling as bright as stars,
Oh, the snow it feels so soft and thick,
As calm as a beautiful dream.

My cheeks are bright red with coldness,
I think I've got frostbite in my toes,
There's my mum, she's calling me,
So night-night snow.

Krystina Dixon (9)

THE NEW GIRL

I am the new girl at Summerfield School
Everyone thinks the deputy head is really cool.

Mr Farley is his name
I think he would do alright on the Generation Game.

My teacher is called Miss Bright.
At first she gave me a terrible fright,
But I soon settled down
And got rid of my frown.
I wish I could say the same about Mr Brown.

Every Monday we go swimming at Bramley Baths
It makes a change from doing maths.

Cross-stitching is not my thing
But oh boy, can I sing!

One day I made an Indian pot
And now I'm learning about cold and hot.
The headteacher is called Mrs Barley
She is a bit like Jacob Marley,
Work, work, work, that's all we do.
No time to rest.
You've got to do another test!

They say my handwriting is too small,
I'll just have to buy a bigger pencil, that's all!

Hannah Barran (8)

THE AUTUMN WEATHER

It's a miserable day
With the wind whipping
Crispy brown leaves off the tree.
They float to the ground like a cradle rocking,
Then land on the moistened earth
With their baby friends.
The sun is hibernating
In its nest of clouds,
Asleep for its long wait till summer,
So it can watch over
The children playing and having fun.

Clouds all soft, fluffy, white,
Like untrodden snow
In the rough, wild, whipping wind.
Boys and girls with kites
Like huge Chinese dragons,
Swirling their tails
In the air.
Wind is ripping leaves off the tree,
Like scraps of torn paper scattered
All over the floor.
Leaves are brown, yellow, gold,
Crunchy cheese and onion crisps.

Paul Southey (11) & Ryan Kalla (10)

WINTER

Winter is a white lion racing through the wood,
His icy mane covering his head just like a hood,
As he roars he turns things to ice,
And kills all creatures such as tiny mice.

His claws are sharp and tail is long,
The birds don't sing their lovely song,
Blue are his eyes which make you shiver,
As he storms across the icy river.

Jessica Adams (10)

A WALK TO THE SHOP

I was walking down the road
On a journey to the shop
And when I got back
I got a big *shock!*

The reason I had a shock
Was because my parents had a lock
They put it on my room
And it was very gloomy!

Then I went to bed
I had a scary dream
I got eaten by a shark
And screamed, scream, scream!

Olivia Cantillon (9)

ANGELS

Angels are there for when you need care,
Or when you're feeling blue.
They're high in the sky playing their harps.
They're above me and you.
They're walking around all day wondering where they could be.
They're probably helping a little kid's cat that is stuck up a tree.
But all I know is that my angel is there and she will always care for me.

Rebecca Kerfoot-Davies (10)

THE MOON

The moon is dark and dingy,
Visited by courageous, heroic astronauts,
The beautiful moonlight whisked in our air,
Admired for centuries by prophets,
Worshipped for decades by wise men,
A deserted, lonely planet,
Small but huge, huge but small,
It's papery white,
Unusually it comes out at night,
It is such a pretty sight,
Like a kite,
Cratered and cold,
The moon is dark and dingy.

Ayeesha Graham (9)
Beaver Road Primary School, Manchester

NIGHT AND MOONLIGHT

Darkness is falling all around
night is nearly touching the ground
scary ghosts in an old house
what was that? Oh, it's just a mouse
dogs howling and cats miaowing
trees with gloomy faces towering
moon is making a silvery light
one young child having a fright
bats flying in the sky
darkness saying goodbye.

Ellen Baines (9)
Brilley CE Primary School, Herefordshire

THE ATTIC

In Pompeii there is a house,
not any ancient Roman house,
a ghost house.
The spirits of the esuvius.

Go past the Acropolis,
see the sights;
go into the streets,
switch on the street lights.

Then you will see it,
a temple of gold;
the ghost died while praying,
in the days of old.

Go into the attic,
on the praying stone;
you might see a flicker,
or a pile of bones.

Daniel Case (9)
Brilley CE Primary School, Herefordshire

DONKEY POEM

Eeh orh goes the donkey's bray,
There he stands and there he'll stay,
Slowly champing the short green grass,
People stare at him when they pass,
He likes to drink from his trough,
It never ever seems enough.

Jessica Jones (10)
Brilley CE Primary School, Herefordshire

MOVEMENT OF THE SKY

The sea-blue sky,
With the mist so high,
The mysterious rain cloud,
Looking innocent and proud.

The calm fireball,
Every night it shall fall,
For then the moon
Will shine like a silver spoon.

In the dark making bright,
The coal-black sky of the hushed mute night,
All is dumb,
And still and numb.

Until the morn,
The sun will be reborn,
Shining blinding beams of light,
Making all a beautiful sight.

Phil Hyde (11)
Brilley CE Primary School, Herefordshire

MY HAMSTER

My hamster is a dancer
he plays in his wheel
and always eats his meal.
He plays in his ball and
crashes into the wall.
He plays with his friends
and the fun never ends
with my hamster
The Dancer.

Ben Morris (10)
Brilley CE Primary School, Herefordshire

WINTER SEASON

The air is brushing through the trees.
The cold, frosty air comes to your door.
The frosty air slithers through my hands.
The gleam of ice on the rivers.

Jake Vaughan (9)
Brilley CE Primary School, Herefordshire

MY FAVOURITE THING IN THE WORLD

My favourite thing in the world,
Is not riding in the car,
Nor dressing up in bangles,
Or to dream of a land afar.

Climbing a tree right up to the sky,
Is not my cup of tea.
Sailing down the river rapid,
Isn't really for me.

Surfing the web in my front room,
Can sometimes be a bore.
In the land of comic strips,
Or watching final score.

Eating dinner, breakfast, lunch,
And reading Harry Potter,
Running round the playing field,
Can really be a rotter.

My favourite thing in the world,
Is definitely not at school,
It's just sitting in a comfy chair
And doing nothing at all.

Louise Bungay (10)
Brynhafren CP School, Powys

MARS - THE PLANET OF WAR

It was a disgusting sight,
soldiers were fighting, killing each other.
It looked like they were getting ready to demolish Mars.
I could hear people shouting and volcanoes erupting
And blowing out fire.
I saw that the ground was turning into boiling lava.
The thunder rumbled and rumbled,
I saw that it was getting dark,
I heard people dying.
The fighting stopped,
but the ground was covered in blood.
Mars - the planet of war.

Daniel Hughes (9)
Brynhafren CP School, Powys

WINTER NIGHTS

Winter nights dark and cold,
now the year is very old,
like a black sheet over the sky,
twinkling stars that never die,
mud is crispy under my feet,
lights are on in the street,
gusts of wind blow my hair,
out alone,
I don't dare.

Twigs tap on windows in the dark,
there's no one playing in the park,
time for bed, I have to go,
but in the morning there might be snow!

James Wolstenholme (9)
Brynhafren CP School, Powys

THE JOURNEY

The sky was light blue,
the boat glided through the calm sea,
there were no clouds to be seen.
Then black soared across the sky,
a raging storm broke,
the thunder was like Cyclops in a rage,
a sea monster was staring at us,
the waves were whipping us.
I always wondered what a slave felt like,
now I knew,
we were slaves to the sea.

I could hear screams from the nearest island,
Zeus was throwing lightning at us,
he was in a rage,
'Help us Poseidon!'

The sea monster started to growl,
the black sky disappeared in a flash,
blue sky again,
the sun sailed through the sky,
the black clouds banished,
there were no fingers of Hades,
calm returned.

The waves stopped whipping us
and became peaceful,
no Cyclops roaring.
Zeus wasn't laughing at us
like Hades' dark fingers.
We were back home with our family -
Poseidon had saved us.
What an adventure!
What an incredible journey.

Gemma Botley (9)
Brynhafren CP School, Powys

THE CITY

In the city I think of statues and flats,
huge parks with massive trees and casinos,
lots and lots of money,
millions of people.

The towers are like big giants,
the TV aerials are like hairs off the giants,
the aeroplanes are like golden eagles roaring through the air,
trains running underground rattling the earth,
cars are like rats creeping up the roads in the dark night
and the statues turfing up the earth
like an earthquake in the dark, dark night.

Matthew Williams (8)
Brynhafren CP School, Powys

A GHOST

I saw a ghost in the corridor
and he looked at me through the door,
he ran away - but that was okay.

The very next day I saw him again
and he looked at me
through the window pane,
'Come, follow me!' he said,
'Come and see!'
And there I was, a hundred ghosts
. . . and me.

Charlie Weaver (7)
Brynhafren CP School, Powys

A Spectacular Journey

We went off in the car
Where were we going?
Are we going to post some mail?
Are we going to a car boot sale?

I wonder, is a museum nearby?
Are we paying a visit in the sky?
My head is burning hot, where are we going?
Come on, come on, I'm waiting.

Are we going to Newcastle?
Are we going to Villa?
Yes of course, now I know,
We're going to watch a thriller.

'No we're not,' said Mum. 'We're going some place new,'
'Oh wonderful, can I please come in too?'
My brother and me were delighted to find out in the end
Suddenly we arrived at the airport to fly to Poland.

Jack Lloyd (10)
Brynhafren CP School, Powys

South Africa

South Africa is lovely and it shines like a diamond
and it's like a desert too.
The shops are dirty,
there was a bomb in our town,
so we ran for our lives up and down,
up and down and up and around,
up the hill and back around.
Africa is like a desert sometimes.

Tom Broom (7)
Brynhafren CP School, Powys

My Favourite Way To Travel

My favourite transport's not a plane,
Or a boat that sails the seven seas,
Or a car that drives in the rain,
Or the back of a swarm of bees.

I really don't like skateboarding,
Or rollerblading freely,
Or a ride on a donkey (that's boring),
Or on a bike doing a wheelie.

It's not a helicopter,
Or a rocket to the moon,
Or a ride on a mucky tractor,
Or flying on a broom.

I wouldn't like a lorry,
Or a milk float full of milk,
I can't fit in a trolley,
And I haven't got wings of silk.

No, all I like to do,
Is sit on my office chair,
Switch the computer on,
And surf the net there.

Kimberley Williams (11)
Brynhafren CP School, Powys

Pet Panic

I wonder which pet I'll buy.
Maybe a dog that can bark and be fun,
Or maybe a bird that can fly.

I wonder which pet I'll choose,
A pet hamster that runs in a ball,
But with a pet I can't lose.

I wonder which pet I'll select,
A fish can be quite boring,
But with a canary I might get pecked!

I wonder which pet I'll purchase,
A pet that I'll play with and love,
I'm sure it will bring a smile to my face.

Sacha Molin (10)
Brynhafren CP School, Powys

THE MAN WHO INVENTED FRACTIONS

The man who invented fractions,
Is my worst enemy,
They are *so* boring,
I bet his name is Jeremy.

I mean, what sort of number is 2/8,
It's just some silly number,
You know what I mean,
Like living in a cucumber.

When it comes to a fraction lesson,
I sink under the table,
I never get it right,
Like finding the fraction of a label!

When we've finished I'm so happy,
I just dance with joy,
Oh no, I don't know what's coming next,
My mum's bought me a fractions toy!

Adam Hilditch (10)
Brynhafren CP School, Powys

DREAMING

Sailing across the moonlit sky,
Come on girls, it's time to fly,
Up and under, over and out,
That's what flying is all about.

Come on, let's fly to the Eiffel Tower,
Let's tell the boys about girl power,
Swinging around the metal bars,
Swinging round that, you won't get far.

I wonder what it would be like to fly,
Up in the clouds, up so high,
That was the best dream yet,
The best you could ever get.

A witch is what I'm dreaming of,
To fly up in the sky above,
I must have been reading too much Harry Potter,
It won't come true, what a rotter.

Charley Broom (11)
Brynhafren CP School, Powys

SLEEPOVERS

I want a sleepover for my birthday.
Mum says yes, Dad says no
What shall I do?
My brain doesn't know.

I want a sleepover for my birthday
Charlotte says yes, Millie says no
What shall I do?
My brain doesn't know.

At last they say yes
After all that struggle,
Then they go and fall out,
Now I'm in a muddle.

Rachel Kelton (9)
Brynhafren CP School, Powys

TO MY UTTER SURPRISE

To my utter surprise,
I saw through my eyes,
The glimpse of a carpet,
But I did not start it.

It flew above my head,
Lifting me from my bed,
Taking me to a far-off place,
Might be up to space.

It took me to Finland,
Germany, France and Poland,
Taking me across the Atlantic Ocean,
Landing in America in commotion.

I travelled around the towns,
Laughing at some clowns,
It's time to return,
Back to my home.

On my way home,
I needed to use a phone,
When I got to the door,
I waved goodbye and said no more.

Millie Andrews (10)
Brynhafren CP School, Powys

RAGING RAPIDS

Raging rapids, splish, splash,
This must be my weekly wash,
Two different passageways, where shall we go?
Come on, let's go left, row.
Missed the rock,
There goes my sock.

I wish I was back home,
In a bath of hot foam,
I miss my warm bed,
And my rabbit Fred.

Down a great big waterfall,
I wish I had my ball,
All the soft white foam,
I wish I was back home,
Zooming past big boulders,
I shrug my shoulders.

Bumping, bumping, all the way,
This is a nervous day,
Come on, we're nearly there,
Look there goes a bear,
Thank goodness it's all over,
Let's go home via Dover.

Stephen Harrison (9)
Brynhafren CP School, Powys

THE CITY

Cars like rats,
windows are eyes,
the colour of skin,
the pipes are tails
and miles of legs.

Flats like monsters,
staring at me,
doors like mouths,
people are Lego men,
a moth is playing with them,
trains are snakes,
hissing through the night.

Robert Bungay (8)
Brynhafren CP School, Powys

NEPTUNE

Neptune is surrounded by lots of clouds
There are angels with silver wings
It snows,
Snowmen appear.
There is gold.
It is peaceful on Neptune.
It disappears into a black hole.

Harvey Stringer (8)
Brynhafren CP School, Powys

ANGRY

When I am angry
I go to my bedroom and bury my face in the pillow,
I go pale with rage.
I go downstairs and shout at Mum,
I go outside and roller skate,
Then it begins to rain,
I run inside and say, 'Sorry.'

Sian Santry (7)
Brynhafren CP School, Powys

SUMMER DREAMS

Sitting on the beach,
Catching a really cool tan,
Lovely and sizzling hot,
Where's the ice cream van?

Lazing in the garden,
Watching the world go by,
Splashing in the paddling pool,
White clouds passing in the sky.

Getting ready to go and party,
With a lovely tan,
Putting all our make-up on,
With my brother Dan.

Having a BBQ in the yard,
With music in my ears,
Beefburgers, sausages and bread,
My dad's drinking loads of beers.

The end is coming nearer,
We're all getting new shoes,
The fun is out of sight,
And here come back our dull school blues.

Alison Hughes
Brynhafren CP School, Powys

LIFE FROM INSIDE A GOLDFISH BOWL

Inside the class goldfish bowl what does the goldfish think?
He might be scared with all the noise and people.
He might think we are giants
With funny shaped heads.
Perhaps it's too light for him or maybe too dark.

When we all go home it is quiet and he can go to sleep.
But soon it's morning and it all starts again.
The only break he gets is at the weekend when everything is still.
He gets his only holiday to the teacher's window sill.

Lucy Edwards (9)
Brynhafren CP School, Powys

THE MAGIC BOX

I will put in the box
A song from a bird that sings a beautiful song
And a tooth to tell your fortune
I will also put a colour from every rainbow
I will put in my box
A snowman from Jamaica
A dragon's tail point
And some water from the bluest stream
I will put in my box
The chant of charming snakes
A fish from every sea
And a cloud from every sky
I will put in my box
The smell of strawberry jam
The taste of apple pie
And a hair strand from every person

My box is green, blue and red
And it has stars and moons and planets.

Claire Keith (10)
Carr Manor Primary School, Leeds

THE MAGIC BOX

I will put in my box
A wide smile on a swaying seal
Ice from an awful, angry ape
Talking teeth from a torturing tiger.

I will put in my box
Thousands and millions of raindrops erupting from a volcano
Snowmen built in Peru!
A kind, gentle, pretty lion.

I will put in my box
Snow falling from the sky in July
The sun shining bright at midnight
An Egyptian man discovering tombs, a baby boy burping.

Being sucked into the box with a gust of wind
Seeing magical lands full of volcanoes
Snowmen when you visit Peru
Talking teeth from a tiger
All in this magical, wonderful box!

Priyen Limbachia (10)
Carr Manor Primary School, Leeds

MY EXPERIENCE OF BONFIRE NIGHT

The big, bright fire burns tonight,
Fireworks make loads of light,
Large ones are an awesome sight,
That we will all view tonight.

Jacket potatoes everywhere,
Their smells floating in the air,
But I do not really care,
Because I am riding on the fair.

I'm spinning round like a Catherine wheel,
Although the waltzers don't make me squeal,
The fire burns more orange peel,
And super is just how I feel.

Alex Baron (10)
Carr Manor Primary School, Leeds

THE MAGIC BOX

   I will put in the box
the heart of a fly,
tiny teeth from an alien T-rex,
a cold volcano from the Arctic.

   I will put in the box
a black white board,
an ancient Egyptian playing a violin,
an Englishman wrapping dead people
in bandages to make them into mummies.

   I will put in the box
a mean, masculine monster that has meningitis,
sparkling, shiny sparks from a sparkler,
a destructive, dangerous dragon.

   I shall look in the box
until I find something else unusual to put in the box.
When I do
I will go back to a magical land in the magic box.

Tiffany Hussain (10)
Carr Manor Primary School, Leeds

My Box

I will put in the box
the whirling, whooshing, wild wind whistling,
the rushing, rapid, rippling river,
swishing, swelling, swirling sound of the sea.
I will put in the box
a lion flicking his mane about whilst roaring,
the leaping frogs on the bouncing lilies,
also a spark of a unicorn's flame.
I will put in the box
a colour of the sunset in a jar,
and a fish in a bed singing,
also a silver sun.
I will put in my box
a bear on the hot, warm sun,
also a witch on a donkey,
and lots of dogs on brooms.

Elizabeth Dishman (10)
Carr Manor Primary School, Leeds

I Listen And I Hear . . .

Crash, roar, shout, cheer, crack, growl, scream and screech.
I listen and I can hear . . .

The loud roar of an angry lion,
The loud cheer of the lively audience,
The loud crash of the angry waves,
The crack of the delicate egg,
The sharp screech of a cat's squeal,
The loud scream from the girls and boys,
The cracking creaking of the big brown door,
I listen and I hear quiet, silence!

Harshna Karsan (8)
Carr Manor Primary School, Leeds

THE MAGIC BOX

    I will put in the box
A big, bright, beady eye of a Beagle
The crinkly claws of an eagle
Fur from a dinosaur

    I will put in the box
Large teeth from a fish
Scale from a slimy singing slug
Sweet song from a bird

    I will put in the box
Rusty rainbow coloured raindrops
A young snowman from the hottest place
An old tiger tooth from a shark

My box is fashioned in chocolate and copper
Sparkling silver, shimmering sequins on the side
Peek inside for a super surprise.

Rachel Bailey (9)
Carr Manor Primary School, Leeds

I LISTEN

I listen and I hear . . .
Crack! Pop! Cheer! Bang! Crash! Thud! Clank!
The big bang of a giant base drum
The horrifying crash of a metal bin falling
The ear-aching cheer of a happy audience
The loudest thud of a gigantic giant's steps
The loud crashing of a big car thrown onto a scrap heap.

I listen and hear
Quiet! Silence!

Thomas Lainchbury (7)
Carr Manor Primary School, Leeds

MY MAGIC BOX

I will put in the box
An African anaconda absailing,
Some small sausages sizzling,
Limping lion lapping up milk.

I will put in my box
A flame of a dragon,
A roar of a lion,
A stripe of a tiger.

I will put in the box
A newborn baby,
An old grandmother,
A boy and a girl.

I will put in the box
Ten purple moons,
A leaf of a blue tree,
A shiny blue house.

My box is red with a violet lid,
My box has stars on top,
My box is full of secrets.

Laura Hudson (9)
Carr Manor Primary School, Leeds

THE MAGIC BOX

I will put in the box
A slithering slimy snake
A colourful rainy rainbow
Creeping, crawling mini spiders
Battered bent books

I will put in the box
A cold shivering sun
Fish on a beach
Clouds in the sea
Starlight in the day.

Sophie Dixon (10)
Carr Manor Primary School, Leeds

MY BOX

　　I will put in the box
the swishing, swooshing, splashing sound of the sea
the frightful flames from the flaming bonfire
the jaws of a jostling jaguar grabbing a giraffe

　　I will put in the box
a dragon with a boiling, flaming belly
a hair from a giant grizzly bear
a fin from a super swimming dolphin

　　I will put in the box
a very long joke in French
a tall, slim pencil
a big fat pencil case

　　I will put in the box
a metal iron bath duck
a live door
a big brown rubber owl

My box is made from thick transparent glass
with silver sequins on top
the lid is made from hard steel
the lock is made from rubber with a bright yellow key.

Graham Matthews (10)
Carr Manor Primary School, Leeds

THE MAGIC BOX

I will put in the box
A lot of rain rushing down,
Runners running in swimming suits,
Swimmers swimming in swimming suits.

I will put in the box
A royal rich sultan in his castle,
A wild adventurous jungle full of animals,
A plane going to China.

I will put in the box
A dirty, slimy, slithery slug,
A lazy old boring ant,
The voice from a singing bird,
A polar bear's fur.

I will also put
A white sun made of rock,
An orange moon made of fire,
Lions that come from Jupiter,
Mars bars coming from Mars.

That's enough now and there's a lot of stuff,
So next time I find a magic box, I'll get extra more!

Manveer Batebajwe (10)
Carr Manor Primary School, Leeds

FIRST TIME FISHING

I remember fishing, fishing
Smelling, hearing, looking
Like a tiger waiting for its prey
Waiting to pounce, pounce

I remember casting, casting
Diving, soaring, plunging, plopping
Like a seagull diving for the fish
The fish

I remember the fish, fish
Gleaming, shining in zigzag patterns
Like a diamond sparkling
So shiny
Shiny

I remember the waves, waves
White, crashing, bashing
Like horses with white manes flying
Galloping, galloping

Then home to lunch
For salad and salmon
Salmon.

Twm Jones (9)
Clyro Church In Wales Primary School, Powys

MY CAT

I remember her hunts
Eyes wide and bright
Ears twitching
Crouched
Then pounce
Like a leaping, roaring wave
Scratching, tearing, ripping
In a flurry of fur and feathers.

I remember her returning
Miaowing quietly
As if to say
'Take me in,
Take pity on me.'
Standing outside
Cold and wet.

I remember her sleeping
By the fire
Curled up with me
Sleeping . . .
  Purring . . .
    Sleeping.

Eleanor Pattison (10)
Clyro Church In Wales Primary School, Powys

MY PET MOUSE

I remember the cage
The cage
Hundreds of mice here and there
All curled into one
And standing on his back legs was
One - a special one
'That one, that one,' I said
'That one.'

I remember the warmth
The warmth
As I touched his soft, black, white-black fur
'George, George, that's his name
George!'

I remember two years on
Two years on
Rushing to play with my friend
'George, George,' I said
He didn't wake!
He was lying all snuggled up
Still
Still.

Josh Pattison (10)
Clyro Church In Wales Primary School, Powys

THE FUNERAL

I remember the sadness
the crying.
Walking round like
speechless ghosts
crying, weeping
and sobbing.

I remember the hoping
the praying
that he would go to
a better place
shivering unhappily
unhappily shivering.

I remember the cold
while holding a holy
prayer book.

I remember the chocolate
receiving it without
enough happiness
to smile or say
thank you
for this was
a death day
and a sad one
too.

Billy Trigg (10)
Clyro Church In Wales Primary School, Powys

AUTUMN

I remember the colours
The colours
Reds, greens, oranges and all
Swirling, swirling all around
Then landing, landing.

I remember the wind,
The wind,
Carrying leaves and
Taking them for leaf rides
All around the park
And stopping, stopping
Where they want to be, be.

I remember the sky
The sky
The grey trapping blueness
So it couldn't come and shine
To greet day
Blue always hidden
Never coming again, again.

I remember the fire
The fire
Raw hands against flaming dancers
Trying to make me stay
I wouldn't leave but I enjoyed it
Enjoyed it.

Bethan Eckley (10)
Clyro Church In Wales Primary School, Powys

SUMMER IN PEMBROKESHIRE

Worn out, I remember the sea,
The sea,
Splashing about, a boy in a pool,
Swimming like an Olympic champion.
I remember diving,
Diving in.

I remember the beach,
The beach,
Standing in the sand.
Bathing in the sand.
Climbing up silky dunes,
Climbing.

I remember the sun,
The sun.
The warmth dazzling down,
Burning in its hot beams.
The heat between two
Weary feet,
After hours . . . worn out
And home.

***Thomas Griffiths (9)
Clyro Church In Wales Primary School, Powys***

SPRING

I remember the buds,
The buds.
Growing, twisting, bursting, splitting,
Twisting like an old tree against the steady years.
Non-stop work, growing through the days,
And twisting,
Twisting.

I remember the pond,
The pond.
Rippling, singing, dancing, running,
Singing like a robin flying by.
The first frog coming into sight,
And wishing,
Wishing.

I remember the lambs,
The lambs.
Snow-white, challenging, brave, jumping,
Jumping like a rabbit, hopping from a fox.
Still having a lot to learn,
And jumping,
Jumping.

Sophie Green (9)
Clyro Church In Wales Primary School, Powys

REMEMBER ME?

Remember me?
I'm the boy you bullied
Because of my size
I'm the boy you bullied after school
I'm the boy you kicked and beat
I'm the boy that walked away crying

You bullied me with a gang of boys
I was beaten like broken toys
Just because you were older didn't mean
You could beat me all the time

Now I am bigger and I am stronger
I am the boy that planned revenge
Now I am not so quick to cry
I am the boy you beat for four years
Now I am bigger and more confident

I could if I wanted as my gangs
Would do, beat you and kick you
But I held back and gave you
My hand.

Conor Murphy (9)
Darkley Primary School, Co Armagh

HALLOWE'EN

Trick or treating,
children squealing,
fireworks banging and pumpkin trying.

Witches flying,
ghosts crying,
wind howling all night long.

Bats flapping,
sparks dropping,
phantoms rapping,
traps clapping.

Skeletons hanging from the rooftops
costumes on children scary as can be.
Hallowe'en is here, whoopee.

Peter McParland (10)
Darkley Primary School, Co Armagh

WET PLAYTIME

What's the matter?
Such a clatter
Who did batter
Jimmy Jone

Clever children
Such a pair
Good as gold
Nobody bold

Teachers coming
Such a sight
Teachers trembling
With no delight

Shut the door
Clear the floor
What's the matter?
Chitter chatter.

Laura Comiskey (10)
Darkley Primary School, Co Armagh

CREATURES LIKE...

The camel is in the desert
Like a mountain standing alone

The grasshopper is in the grass
Like a piece of paper in the bin

The owl is in the tree
Like a lantern in the night

The salmon in the water
Like an aspirin in a glass of juice.

Jade McConville
Denend Primary School, Fife

CREATURES LIKE

The sheep is in the field,
Like my gran knitting a jumper.

The beetle is on the ground,
Like a blackout in the war.

A buzzard is in the sky,
Like a glider above the hills.

A goldfish in a pond,
Like an orange in a fruit bowl.

Craig Chrisp (11)
Denend Primary School, Fife

CREATURES LIKE . . .

The wolf in its den
Like the wind howling through the night.

The spider on its web
Like a starving tramp.

The owl on the branch
Like a smart guy doing his maths.

The salmon in the water
Like an Olympic gold medallist.

Scott Ormiston (11)
Denend Primary School, Fife

CREATURES LIKE . . .

The rabbit in its hut
Like a teapot on a tray

The ants in their holes
Like sandwiches in their box

The eagle in the sky
Like an aeroplane doing loop-the-loop

The goldfish in a tank on the table
Like meat in its gravy.

Margaret Jamieson (11)
Denend Primary School, Fife

A Jacobite's Wishes

I have a lot of wishes just sitting in my head
I wish for no more war or thick red blood getting spilt
I wish to wake up and smell the fresh air
Not the rotting corpses of my family.
I wish I could practise my own religion
Without fighting for it.
I wish the rightful monarch would take his place
In the throne, not monster King George II!
Please let my prayers be answered.

Ross Halleron (11)
Denend Primary School, Fife

A Jacobite's Wishes

I have a mind full of wishes.
Let me have my family in a safe place
in the forest next to a loch.
Let me hear the leaves rustling on the trees,
the water crashing off the rocks when I wake up.
Stop the Hanoverians from slaughtering women, children and men.
Let us wear tartan and let us play bagpipes.
I hope it all comes true.

Kim McCathie (11)
Denend Primary School, Fife

The Warm And The Cold

A badger in its hole
Like a log on the ground

A butterfly sitting on a tree
Like a girl's ribbon in her hair

An owl wise and still
Like the moon in the sky

A salmon jumping in the river
Like a bouncy ball out of control.

Richard Wood (11)
Denend Primary School, Fife

A JACOBITE'S WISHES

A hae a heed fu o' wishes
Fir a safe, secure home in ma village
Nixt tae a loch.
Tae awaken wi a' body is richt' is rain,
Instid o' hools o' thee injured.
Rocks in pebbles nixt tae lumps o' green griss,
In a the mountains instid o' lairs o' rid blood,
Thit dyed the griss in pebbles fa' in doon aff,
The mountain caused bi the Rid-Coats.

A dinna want a' the Hanovarians ruinin' a' thin',
A' the bairns screamin' thir wee heeds' aff!
Wimin tryin' tae protict the wee yins,
Whin they canno save thir-sels',
If a hid the poowir I'd mak' peace 'n' hirmony,
George II in Charles Edward Stuart kid work oot
Who's gonna be king thir-sels!
Bit still I'm nae poorful so a' canna dae that,
So we hae tae ficht' fir thim!
Well ma hopes ir oot, it at least wan,
Is graunted a'd be gratefu'.

Nicola Shand (11)
Denend Primary School, Fife

A Jacobite's Wishes

I have a mind full of wishes
let me have a warm, cosy, black house in the hillside,
let me have peace in the morning when I wake and hear
children laugh instead of scream in terror,
let me have my family with me and not get in any battles,
let me and my fellow men wear tartan and play out bagpipes,
let Butcher Cumberland keep away,
leave these helpless women and children,
let me see our beautiful countryside instead of the sight
of gory bodies lying on the green grass,
let me have food we need to feed my family,
let the bloodshed stop then we will have less deaths,
maybe one day my dreams will come true.

Michelle Rankin (11)
Denend Primary School, Fife

A Jacobite's Wishes

I have a mind packed with wishes.
I hope one day that I can live in peace and worship how I want.
To live and let live with the Hanoverians.
But now I am here lying on the battlefield with a dirk in my stomach.
Please let the war stop!

William Braid (11)
Denend Primary School, Fife

A JACOBITE'S WISHES

I have a mind full of wishes.
Let me be safe and happy in my peaceful home in the glen.
I would like to wake up to the sound of birds cheeping or
Children playing, not swords clanging and wounded people screaming.
I would give anything to be free from Butcher Cumberland.
It is a terrible sight seeing families turning against each other,
And women and children as white as ghosts
Watching their family dying on the battlefield.
I hope to see no more wars or bloodbaths every time I venture out.
I want my family back but I know that won't happen.
I would give anything to see my beautiful wife and children again.
Well I can only dream.
Things will never be the same again.

Elaine Moyes (11)
Denend Primary School, Fife

A JACOBITE'S WISHES

I wish I lived in the Highlands in a little brick house.
Instead I'm lying injured on the battlefield.
I wish I was warming myself up at the fire
With a warm blanket around me,
Eating smoked fish and going to a nice warm straw bed.
Then in the morning hearing a wake-up song of a bird.
But I will probably die here on the battlefield.

Kimberley Wilson (11)
Denend Primary School, Fife

CHOCOLATE

Yummy, scrummy, nice
I like chocolate mice.
Milky, dark or white,
Do you want a bite?
Wispa, Aero, Galaxy, Mars,
Crunchie, Caramel, Milky Way Stars.

This is a journey of a chocolate bar
I know where it's going and it's not very far.
I'm a food tester.
It's a very important job
And this chocolate bar is going in my gob.

Once it is there
I chew it all up
Then I swallow it
And give some to my pup.

Inside my belly
It turns into jelly
And then, and I don't pretend,
It comes out the other end.

Ed Stockham (11)
Dinas CP School, Pembrokeshire

TILLY'S SILLY SOUNDS

Crocodiles snap
crocodiles nap
Crocodiles' teeth go snap
snap, snap, snap.

Puppies pounce
puppies yap
puppies' paws go bounce
bounce, bounce, bounce.

Kittens play
kitten lay
in the sunshine all the day
lap the milk
lick their paws
lap, lick, lap, lick.

Tilly Macrae (8)
Dinas CP School, Pembrokeshire

DAIRY FARM

D ogs chasing sheep.
A nimals need feeding.
I like the farm.
R abbits on the run.
Y oung animals playing.

F armer on his tractor.
A lways working hard.
R ats killed by Bobby.
M oo! Go the cows.

Michael Evans (11)
Dinas CP School, Pembrokeshire

KITTENS

K ittens are cute
I like them
T ails as furry as its head
T ongue is rough as stone
E yes that glow in the dark
N ails as sharp as needles
S leeps on the stairs.

Rachael Evans (8)
Dinas CP School, Pembrokeshire

UNTITLED

Ten brand new Subarus on the starting line
one failed to start the race and then there were nine.

Nine brand new Subarus trying not to be late
one ran out of petrol then there were eight.

Eight brand new Subarus on their way to Devon
one got lost on the way and then there were seven.

Seven brand new Subarus got into a fix
one slid off the track and then there were six.

Six brand new Subarus going for a drive
one had a puncture and then there were five.

Five brand new Subarus with numbers on the door
one engine blew up and then there were four.

Four brand new Subarus didn't see the tree
one banged into it then there were three.

Three brand new Subarus, one caught the flu
sneezed and crashed and then there were two.

Two brand new Subarus, one got a gun
and went out shooting and then there was one.

One brand new Subaru went to find his mum
stayed there for the night and then there were none.

Tom Parkes (9)
Dinas CP School, Pembrokeshire

PLAYFUL DOG

My dog Tramp
Is a Jack Russell.
His nose is damp
And he's got muscle.

His face is brown
His ears are black
He is like a clown
With a white and black back.

He can shake my hand
But I shake his paw
He can do a two-legged stand
And snap his jaw.

He jumps for a bone
And he loves his home
He doesn't roam.

He'll roll across the floor
Like a bowling ball
Through my bedroom door
And runs down the hall.

I like Tramp
He is my dog
He'll jump and stamp
And chase a log.

Mathew Reading (8)
Dinas CP School, Pembrokeshire

MY BROTHER JAMIE

My brother Jamie
he's not a baby
he's grown up
to be a toddler
he likes to play
with his bricks
and he learnt a lot of tricks
he likes a good laugh
and smiles all day
he is a bit annoying
but he's my brother
in every way.

My brother Jamie
he is a big eater
he always goes munch!
Munch! Munch!
Crunch! Crunch!
He likes to eat
a lot of lunch
he likes a good laugh
he smiles all day
he is a bit annoying
but he's my brother
in every way.

My brother Jamie
he likes a good laugh
he smiles all day
he is a bit annoying
but he's my brother
in every way.

Matthew Holmes (9)
Dinas CP School, Pembrokeshire

THE KEY FITS

Trembling
I turned the lock
The door opened quickly
I felt scared
I went in
The door closed
I didn't even touch it
I saw another door
But then something
Spoke to me
I screamed, 'Ahhhh!'
I ran to the door
I went in and
I saw another door
I opened it
I saw a box
I opened the box
It was a treasure
I jumped for joy, yippee
I carried as much treasure
As I could
Through the haunted room
Back out the door
I was safe and
I was rich.

Fiona McKechnie (9)
Ferguslle Primary School, Renfrewshire

YELLOW

Yellow is the sunshine
Shining very bright,
Yellow is a fire
Shining like a light.
Yellow is the colour
Of a bruise,
Or even the colour
Of pineapple juice.

Louise Bain (9)
Ferguslie Primary School, Renfrewshire

YELLOW

Yellow is the colour of the sun.
We all like to go out and have some fun.
When it goes down we all frown.
The next day when it comes out,
We all jump about.
We all like the sun
Because we all think it's fun.

Kayleigh McCramigle (9)
Ferguslie Primary School, Renfrewshire

COLOURS

Yellow, yellow, bright as the sum.
Yellow-gold is like a currant bun.
Yellow is the colour of daffodils
I gave to my mum on her birthday.
Yellow is the road to Mum's house.

Yellow is the colour of my sweatshirt.
It is also the colour of bananas.
A big yellow taxi I took to town.
Also yellow mixed with blue makes brown.

Laura Leitch (9)
Ferguslie Primary School, Renfrewshire

WHO AM I?

I can swim . . .
My legs are long when I go
Into the water and swim . . .

I can't bite . . .
I can't harm . . .
I can't scare a thing . . .
The only thing I do is swim . . .

I'm just a lonely frog in the pond . . .

Toni Lauchlan (9)
Ferguslie Primary School, Renfrewshire

BLUE

Blue is the colour of the sea.
Blue is for you and me.
Blue is the colour of violets.
Blue is the colour when I'm sad.
Blue is the colour of the sky.
Blue is the colour of my eyes
As I watch the clouds go by.

Kenny Tarbert (9)
Ferguslie Primary School, Renfrewshire

SEASONS OF THE YEAR

Glittery winter snow melting,
Slowly in the town.

Brown autumn leaves hovering wildly
All the way down.

Pink summer flowers blooming
Quickly, looking very fine.

Bronze autumn petals falling softly
Underneath the sunshine.

Glistening ice hardening madly
In the playground.

Crunchy ripped petals drifting
Silently, they make no sound.

Scolding hot days
When children dance happily
Like they do all year round.

Fiery autumn leaves crunch constantly
On the ground.

They are the seasons of the year.

Jade Birkett (9)
Hartside Primary School, Co Durham

THE LIFE OF THE SUN

Fiery light, blinding cruelly
Mystery ball eclipses slowly
Yellow sphere burning strongly
Without the sun all life would be extinct.

Danny Parker-Brooks (9)
Hartside Primary School, Co Durham

THE SUN

Mysterious ball of fire burning brightly each day,
Yellow sphere rises quickly in the morning sky,
Shiny beams blaze fiercely when it rises,
Strong rays sparkle magically in the afternoon,
Red star shines daily in the blue sky,
Bright lights blind painfully if you look at it,
The sun has gone down and it is the end of the day.

Paul Harvey (8)
Hartside Primary School, Co Durham

I'M DREAMING OF A WHITE WINTER

White snow glittering mystically,
Blanketing slowly through the night.
Silver balls of snow falling fast,
While holiday travellers take their flight.
But I like it here all cold and grey,
So I can go out to play and play.

Ruth Cranston (9)
Hartside Primary School, Co Durham

THE HOT SPOT

Scalding hot sun rises quickly in the morning
The sparkling shine burns dangerously
Bronze star rises slowly every day
Scalding sunset sets madly every evening
Mysterious blinding ball of fire.

Antony Howcroft (8)
Hartside Primary School, Co Durham

SUNNY DAYS

Orange sun rises daily
In the red sky,
Fiery sphere burns brightly
In the afternoon,
Red beams blind strongly
As its face grins,
Mysterious star sets slowly
As its rays shine out.

Josh Craig (9)
Hartside Primary School, Co Durham

THE SUN'S LIFE

The yellow burning star fiercely eclipses the moon,
Misty flashes of heat appear at noon,
Its smiling face suddenly hides away,
It is night now and it's the end of the day.

Rebecca Anderson (9)
Hartside Primary School, Co Durham

THE WINTER WONDERLAND

Milky snowman falling softly to the ground.
Smooth fog floating tenderly in mid-air.
White snowball sliding quickly onto the pavement.
Icy slush hardening dangerously in the yard.

Hayley Walton (8)
Hartside Primary School, Co Durham

WINTER WONDERLAND

Tingly snow melting slowly
Milky sheet glowing softly
Slippery slush sliding madly
Foggy winter glittering magnificently
Icy snow freezing dangerously
Smooth frost covering recently,
Silvery ice hardening magically,
Along your window sill.

Nathan Gilchrist (9)
Hartside Primary School, Co Durham

WINTER LOCATION

Milky sheet of glistening snow,
Covered all over the earth like a blanket,
I pick a snowball up and I get frostbite
A silver snowman slumped on the ground.

Hayley Trotter (9)
Hartside Primary School, Co Durham

SNOWFLAKES

Cold snow glittering like diamonds
Covering the earth as we sleep
Soft silken flakes floating
Down the valley so deep.

Sarah Clarey (8)
Hartside Primary School, Co Durham

WINTER DAY

Cold ice freezing slow in the winter
White snow falling quickly down from the sky
Glittering fog sparkling magnificently
Milky snowman melting into a heap
At the end of the day.

Anthony Conley (8)
Hartside Primary School, Co Durham

THE ICY LAND

Lovely glittery snowdrops that fall onto the floor.
You can make a snowman and so, so much more.
Don't get in a huff if it falls down.
We can make another one if it's on the ground.

Charmaine O'Brien (9)
Hartside Primary School, Co Durham

WINTER DAYS

Glittery ice smashing roughly in the day.
Cold rain raining, magically it's going away.
Hard snow melting quickly by my sight.
Mysterious mist fading slowly in the night.

Laura Hook (9)
Hartside Primary School, Co Durham

A COLD WINTER'S DAY

A cold winter's snowy day, so cold,
Silvery white falling to the ground,
So slippery and grey, hard to hold,
As it falls to the ground without a sound,
Crystal clear snowdrops dropping from the sky,
Rapidly throwing snowballs
But thank God we can go to sleep.

Laura Winter (8)
Hartside Primary School, Co Durham

WHERE IS IT?

Oh where is it?
I hear rustling
Oh no, I sense it
But I cannot see it.

I hear its roar
My heart is beating faster
I feel its movements
I hear a shuffle
But I cannot see it.

What was that?
I did not like it
I feel frightened
I want to go home
Ahhggghhha!
It got me.

Lesley Seddon (9)
Kingsway Primary School, Merseyside

A Nail Biter

A nail-biter
A vicious fighter

A long-sleeper
A sneaky-creeper

A hungry beast
A huge feast

A prey-catcher
A mean-snatcher

A catalogue to make me
A lion.

Nadia Forbes (10)
Kingsway Primary School, Merseyside

Seaside Poem

S   un is shining on the beach
E   agles flying in the sky
A   nglers are fishing in the sea
S   wimming, swimming
I   n the sea
D   ucking under the water
E   very day, by the seaside.

Danielle Morgan (9)
Kingsway Primary School, Merseyside

MY PLAYFUL GINGER CAT

My playful ginger cat
She is really very fat,
She always sits by the fire on the mat
My cat hangs around me like a nat.

My playful ginger cat
Loves to eat my food,
She scratches me when she's in a mood
She loves to climb all over me.

My playful ginger cat
She jumps like a frog,
And loves to tease our dog.
She hides from me in the fog
And snuggles at the bottom of my bed.

Corinne Upton (10)
Kingsway Primary School, Merseyside

DECEMBER MORNING

White snow
in the wintertime
carol singers at the door
presents under the tree for Christmas Day
in the snow.

Daniel Sanders (10)
Kingsway Primary School, Merseyside

A LOUD KILLER

A bird-eater.
A bird-cheater.

A super swimmer.
A loud killer.

A fluffy tail.
A scratching nail.

A red coat.
A billy goat.

A huge-trapper.
A big snapper.
A catalogue to make me a fox.

Zoe Dalton (10)
Kingsway Primary School, Merseyside

SPACE

Up in space is a different world,
Satellites float and galaxies curl.
UFOs dance in the sky,
All until morning is nigh.
Stars flicker, moon shines,
The sky is full of different signs.
Venus comes and goes again,
At night all the stars and planets rise.
It's a different place up in space.

Dayle Dunlop (9)
Kingsway Primary School, Merseyside

THE INVISIBLE BEAST

The beast sounds really scary,
It might be in your own school,
You don't know where it is,
It might be in your swimming pool.

I really want to go to my house,
I'm walking through the park,
I'm in for a big surprise,
And I can't see it even though it's not dark.

I try to run home
To a safer place,
But I am too nervous,
I need to find a phone.

Michaela Carson (9)
Kingsway Primary School, Merseyside

THE INVISIBLE BEAST

The invisible beast
Right behind
I cannot see it
I have lost my mind
Glad am not in the park
Though it isn't very dark
I am very scared
Soon I hear someone appear
It might be someone dancing really cool
Or it might be a swimming pool
I cannot see it
'But maybe it can see me!'

Samantha Carr (8)
Kingsway Primary School, Merseyside

TEA WITH SPOOKS

Tea with spooks is no delight,
Their favourite time is night.
We have such fun at Hallowe'en,
It really makes my face turn green.

Hallowe'en, Hallowe'en,
It really makes me want to scream.
Now I want to run with fright,
Before the spooks come out tonight.

Now I hear the spooky sound,
Spooks dance all around.
Ghosties boogie woogie,
I shake and shoogie.

Suddenly I hear a shout saying, 'Come out!'
Slowly I crawl from my den with a shout.
To find spooks watching me,
All holding cups of tea!

Rebecca Fleming (10)
Larbert Village Primary School, Stirlingshire

CHOCOLATE CAKE

My nan makes it taste delicious,
I never like to stop eating it.
So special, I eat it all the time,
When I eat too much I feel sick.
It's moist and delicious,
And it's all for me!

Rachael Gwilt (9)
Lindridge CE Primary School, Worcestershire

SEASONS

Bushy trees full of colourful leaves,
Conkers get smashed one by one,
Children are all having lots of fun,
A colourful season for everyone!

Flakes of snow are coming down,
Snowmen are standing in a row,
Children all wish the snow would not go,
The season is cold, everyone should know!

Flowers are just starting to open,
The grass is starting to grow,
Everybody is happy,
It's spring!

Blossoms are blooming again,
Animals come out to have fun,
Children are playing outside,
Look, there's the sun!

Sarah Jones (8)
Lindridge CE Primary School, Worcestershire

AUTUMN

The crisp leaves are crunching under my feet.
The brown twigs are snapping under my feet.
The bright berries are squashing under my feet.
The crackling bonfire is burning my toes.
The dazzling fireflies are whizzing past my nose.
The evil bats are swirling around my clothes.
The glistening full moon has a shadow of a *witch!*

Lucy Wylde (8)
Lindridge CE Primary School, Worcestershire

THE MOON'S VOYAGE ACROSS THE SKY

Step upon step,
The moon walks across the open sky,
Forgotten not.
Swaying in its silver sea,
Hanging from the precious chain of life and age.

The rising moon reveals the creatures of the dark,
And the hidden natures of the world,
The glowing rays bring them to life,
Wrapping its warm caring arms around the world.
A blanket of warmth,
A ceiling of light.
The fierce face of the moon shuns the bright sun.
Rising in the distance,
Glowing sun versus gloomy moon?
The moon grows tired,
It begins to rest,
While the sun awakes,
And begins to rise.

Step upon step,
The moon walks across the open sky,
Forgotten not.
Swaying in its silver sea,
Hanging from the precious chain of life and age,
Ever gone.

Till tomorrow evening,
When the fun begins,
When the precious chain swings!

Tanita Pardoe (11)
Lindridge CE Primary School, Worcestershire

THE JOURNEY OF CHILDHOOD

The journey of childhood,
Is like a time travel through space,
Or a clock ticking away every second,
Like a person growing older and older.

First I'm a baby,
In my mother's arms,
Coming out of hospital,
People say, 'What a charm!'

Second I'm a toddler,
Pulling people's hair,
Trying to take my first step,
But clinging to a chair.

Third I think I'm a big girl,
Learning to talk,
Thinking that I'm taking,
My pet dog for a walk.

Four, I'm in big school,
Learning big sums,
My favourite time is playtime,
When we all skip in the sun.

Now I'm nine,
Nearly ten,
For Christmas my mum,
Brought me a new fountain pen.

The years went by,
I'm married now,
I have two children,
I wonder what tomorrow, the future, will bring.

Tess Champion (9)
Lindridge CE Primary School, Worcestershire

JOURNEY OF LIFE

First days of my life as a baby,
I was screaming and crying all day,
Throwing my food everywhere,
And always wanting to play.
When I was a toddler,
I was pulling everyone's hair,
Giving everyone's shoes to the dog,
I didn't care!
When I grew older,
Every time my birthday came,
I shouted and screamed at every present
And the magician's tricks were really lame.
Because I became a teenager,
I didn't care as much about my birthdays,
I didn't have the magic magicians,
As much as I did in my first days.
In adulthood I was getting a job,
Work, work, work,
Starting to settle down with women,
And finally becoming a clerk.

Thomas Jeffrey (10)
Lindridge CE Primary School, Worcestershire

THE FOX

The fox is stalking its wild prey,
Instead of night, he does it in the day,
The vixen is sleeping in her den,
The cubs are in the chicken pen.

The badger will come out at night,
It really is a beautiful sight,
The buzzards are circling up above
So are the pigeons and the turtle dove.

The deer are brown with black antlers,
The big, wise reindeer are Santa's,
They fight at Scotland on the moors,
They take a drink from the shores.

David Sherriff (8)
Lindridge CE Primary School, Worcestershire

THE JOURNEY TO WALK

I tried to walk
But I fell.
I bumped my head and cried.
I tried again and I did it.
I danced all over the place.
Mummy and Daddy said something I did not know,
But I could see they were happy.
I did what I had thought
I'd never complete,
I walked my first step.

Charlotte Ginger (10)
Lindridge CE Primary School, Worcestershire

I SAW A BIRD

I saw a bird upon a tree.
I saw a bird flying free.
I heard a bird singing sweet.
I saw it fly away to meet
Another bird that was oh singing sweet.

Michelle Hargreaves (8)
Lindridge CE Primary School, Worcestershire

SNOW

Snow is falling on the ground,
Glistening and twinkling all around.

Snow is falling from the sky,
I hope it won't be too high.

So I play in the snow hoping it will never go,
Tired and wet, cold and blue.

It's off home to bed to snuggle up
And get warm through.

Leigh Hanson (8)
Lindridge CE Primary School, Worcestershire

AUTUMN

Autumn leaves going round and round,
Leaves are going down and down,
Autumn leaves make a sound,
Leaves are falling in the town.

Autumn turns to winter,
Every person is getting ready,
Father Christmas is waiting and he is near.

Louise Potter (8)
Lindridge CE Primary School, Worcestershire

THE SKY

The sky at day lets me play.
The clouds they move freely they say.
Feel the sun with its warming glow
Helping trees and plants grow.

The sky at night gives me a fright,
So black and dark, hear those dogs bark.
The moon it shines so clear and bright,
Helps me to see the owl in flight.

Joel Brook (8)
Lindridge CE Primary School, Worcestershire

DOGS

Dogs are very nice and fluffy,
They'll let you tickle their tummy.
There are Rottweilers and spaniels too,
But the best is Jake my puppy.

Jake is very playful and strong,
He'll round up sheep as quick as you bang a gong.
He likes to take a dip in the pool,
When he gets out he looks very cool.

Joshua Thompson (8)
Lindridge CE Primary School, Worcestershire

THE VOYAGE OF LIFE

Began in 1990, one bright June morn.
Friday the 15th, the day I was born.
The first breath I took was Worcestershire air.
With a head full of dark, not fair hair.
Dad chose my name, Lydia,
Which is a bit like my cousin's name, Olivia.
My eyes of sparkling blue.
Myself not having a clue.
Growing up each day,
Changing in every way.

Lydia Millichap (10)
Lindridge CE Primary School, Worcestershire

THE JOURNEY THROUGH SCHOOL

First I was in class one,
I only did one sum!
My teacher was really nice,
And her teeth chattered like mice!

When I was in class two,
I could tie the lace of a shoe.
All of my teeth started to grow,
And I tied my hair in a bow.

Then I was in class three,
I could hum the sound of a honey bee.
Then I started to write well,
And ring the school bell.

Finally I went into class four,
You had to knock on the door.
We learned about arts,
And lots of different charts!

Penny Sherriff (9)
Lindridge CE Primary School, Worcestershire

BIRDS

Buzzard, thrush, sparrow, crow
I wish I'd seen a dodo
Starling, wagtail, robin, wren
Once they're gone they'll never come again

The swan nests in reeds
A kestrel lives in rocks
Falcons perch on wires
Each one finds what it needs.

William Dayson (7)
Lindridge CE Primary School, Worcestershire

MY BROTHER

In goes the CD
Round and round it spins
What can I hear?
I'm sure that's violins!

The music's getting faster
And someone's singing now
This is my favourite track
It's brilliant! Super! Wow!

Bang! The door flies open
In comes my brother Doug
Turning off *my* music
By yanking out the plug.

I am really angry
And run at him in rage
He's such a little monkey
We should lock him in a cage.

Now I'm on the landing
And trying to grab his arm
Oh no, here comes my mum
She says, 'He's caused no harm.'

I raced back to my bedroom
My tears I had to hide
Is it because he's little
That she always takes his side?

Is my CD ruined?
If it is I'll make him pay
It's good he's out tomorrow
But bad he is at home today.

Joanna Webber (10)
Merstham CP School, Surrey

A TRIP TO SEE MICKEY

Christmas in Disneyworld
What a lovely time for me
Lights up high
How lovely to see
Everything was Christmassy and
Our hearts were filled with glee
Roller coasters up and down
Exciting shows for us to see
Loop the loops and tower of terror
Scared to death were Mum and me
Pooh and the gang
What could be better
Apart from a trip
To see . . . Mickey!

Elizabeth Stanger (9)
Merstham CP School, Surrey

FIREWORKS

Fireworks make a loud noise,
When I have fireworks I play with my toys

I like fireworks, I don't find them boring,
But it is when your next door neighbours are snoring.

Fireworks are bright.
When they go *bang!* they give you a fright.

The Catherine wheel spins round and round,
Rockets are fired from the ground.

Karla-Ann Dauncey (9)
Merstham CP School, Surrey

ANIMALS

Big, small, large, tall
Animals come in all sizes
Fat, thin, long, short
Some that win prizes

Black, white, grey, tan
Every colour known to man
Thick fur, feathers sleek
Covers for the strong and the weak

They're born, they live, but soon they'll die
No longer seen by you or I
Earth gets more polluted every hour
No more animals, no more flowers

Stop dropping litter, causing trouble
For otherwise the mess will double
The Earth will choke and scream in pain
No living things will be seen again

And where would we be without them all?
Fat and thin, big and small
Running, leaping, crawling, hopping
Moving constantly, never stopping

The world will change if we don't stop
This crazy habit of buy, unwrap, drop
Not just for man, but animals too
Stop polluting Earth - and that means *you!*

Katie Ballard (9)
Merstham CP School, Surrey

THE WORLD

Open the door, look at the view,
God has created that for me and you.
Some countries are hot, some countries are cold,
Some people are young, some people are old.
Some places are wet, some places are dry
On this poem I really did try.

The oceans and seas are large and vast
So cast off the ship's white mast.

Countries make large continents
With their own special monuments
So visit them soon
Because they're nearer than the moon.

In the forest there are animals
In the sea there are mammals.
(They are also on land but if I had added it in
It would have sounded stupid and have gone in the bin!)

Different animals roam the land
But the killings of man's hand
Life is stopped for them and
All because of selfish men.

Nature made fruit and veg
To make a healthy diet
But when junk food was made
There was an unhealthy riot.

Tiny birds flew around
Their shadows cast upon ground.
The wet grass from this morning dew
Hide the soggy wet cat mew.

It soon will be the end
Hopefully the Earth is on the mend.
To clear up and get its act together about where we live
That's how you and I will survive in this world we share
                              with God's created animals.

Nathaniel Harper (10)
Merstham CP School, Surrey

MY CAT SUKI

She waits in the morning sitting on the rug
Until I come down and give her a hug
She's black and white and oh so furry
When she sits on my lap she's very purry

Sometimes I brush her shiny fur
And when I do she begins to purr
Her fur is soft, shiny and clean
And has such a lovely sheen

Sometimes she can be a pain
She even goes out in the rain
Then she comes in all wet and soggy
But, I still love my moggy.

Laura Jayne Boxall (9)
Merstham CP School, Surrey

A STRESSFUL DAY OF A TEACHER!

Late

You are late for school,
You get out of bed,
Got to comb your hair,
You have banged your head,
You have to look cool so the kids don't joke,
You ate breakfast too fast,
You are going to choke.

Run into your car,
You have ran out of fuel,
Have to hurry to school,
You catch the bus,
Man are you late,
The Head is going to fuss,
You have got a big spot,
It is seeping with puss.

You arrive at school,
The late bell rings,
I am such a fool,
I forgot my things,
I ran to class and taught the kids.

The lunch bell rings,
Us staff eat like kings,
I drink my coffee and eat my lunch,
The bell rings once . . . twice, have to get to class.

I taught science,
We dissected mice,
One of my students had headlice,
Time to go home,
This time I walked,
Someone smashed my garden gnomes!

I get in a warm, relaxing bath,
Have some chocolate fudge cake,
And I laugh and think of the day I had,
I slowly climb into bed and drift away from life . . .
The alarm bell rings!

Late.

Alexander Bull (9)
Merstham CP School, Surrey

MY PODGY LITTLE GUINEA PIG

My podgy little guinea pig,
hides under his box all day.
The only time I see him is in the morning
and at the end of the day.
He has very funny habits
like running away from rabbits.
When it comes to the end of the day
I go away and in the hutch,
I give him food and there he stays
until night is through.

Sarah Neil (9)
Merstham CP School, Surrey

SCHOOL

School is a place that nobody likes.
To get there some of us ride bikes.
In class you have loads of tests,
And the teachers always say,
'Get back to work you little pests.'

Luke Cartwright (9)
Merstham CP School, Surrey

MY DREAM

Once I had a dream that pigs could fly,
Once I had a dream that no one could lie,
Once I had a dream that people couldn't cry,
Did you? Did you?
No, neither did I.
Alright then, what do you dream?
I dream of strawberries and cream,
I dream of food that makes you scream,
I dream that salad was a football team,
I dream that there was solid chocolate PE balancing beam.
That's what I dream!

Mitchell Stevens (10)
Merstham CP School, Surrey

RABBITS

Fur like a velvet jacket
Long, soft, creamy ears
Small, fluffy tail
Two tiny legs and two huge thumping legs
Cute, friendly face
Hopping up and down
Nibbling blades of grass each second
Bright sunshine shining on its back
Like glitter on a silver carpet.

Tim Buttle (9)
Merstham CP School, Surrey

AUTUMN

The leaves make all the tall trees bare
Spreading the floor everywhere.
Autumn is making the trees go to sleep
While all the wind begins to peep.
The wind is frosty and cold
The wind is big and bold.
The wind is frosty and chilly too
Who made the wind blow, I wonder who.
The animals are gently sleeping
Until the spring begins peeping.
The sun will rise and spring is here
Until the wind begins to appear.

Darryl Kirby (9)
Merstham CP School, Surrey

THE EAGLE

Swooping in the sky
Wings long, breast high
If you see one, with a flick of an eye
It'll be gone and out of sight.

Soaring on raised wings
Covering miles of moorland and bare hillside
Piercing eyes scanning far and wide
Until the eye picks out a poor and helpless rabbit.

James Trumper (10)
Merstham CP School, Surrey

THE HIGHWAYMAN

There is an old legend still told today,
Though no one alive remembers the truth . . .
That on a night of mystery and gloom,
Whilst mist swirled and churned around,
A tall dark figure waited in silence,
High on a great stamping stallion named Nightmare,
Though the man's name nobody knew,
And wearing his night black cape, was swallowed into darkness,
Just waiting, waiting . . .

Then from out of the darkness, the distant sound of running horses
And squealing coach wheels cut through the night.
The evil form stared at the coach with mean, glistening eyes,
And pulled up his mask, urging his horse on, he shouted words to bring
Fear to all hearts. 'Stand and deliver - your lives or your money!'
For he was a highwayman, out to do evil and harm.
To rob and kill, before slipping eerily into the swirling gloom.

Sarah Bovey (11)
Montbelle Primary School, Kent

WINTER FROST

When winters fall they make a blanket of frost
The air is sour and chilled when all colour is lost
When darkness comes it freezes the air
The trees rattle although they are bare!

Poor animals trying to keep warm
Although no animals can be born
Birds and mice trying to find food
They are not in a very happy mood!

Minus degrees
Freeze the leaves
Cold winds whip the trees
Clouds turn black and very dark
Brown which turns to white crispy bark!

Charlotte Read (10)
Montbelle Primary School, Kent

THE THING FROM THE WOODS

Some people say it's the wind that howls,
But no one can see through the eyes of the owls.
Splashes we hear from the moonlit lake,
Something is out there, but no one's awake.
Blood running down a rotting tree,
Something is out there and it's after me.
Suddenly we hear a scream,
Stopping the noise of the trickling stream.
Through the bushes comes the village queen,
Who starts to tell us what she has seen.
A monster that is so huge and mean,
That even two miles away it still can be seen.
Teeth glinting like the sun,
If you see it don't stand still . . . just run!
Footprints lead to an open door,
Then inside we hear a roar.

Then from the house came a *wolf!*

Kate Elliott (11) & Rebecca Fay-Read (10)
Montbelle Primary School, Kent

WINTER

Snowflakes falling on the ground,
Happy children all around.
Jack Frost on the window panes,
Stoke up the fire into some flames.

The snowflakes make a blanket of white,
It is a wonderful and beautiful sight.
Snowflakes sparkling in the sky,
Cold, white swans flying by.

Icicles hanging from the trees,
'Quick, get in, before you freeze.'
The candlelight is burning bright,
On this frosty, winter's night.

Little robin trying to keep warm,
From this blustery and snowy storm.
He puts his head under his wing,
Just then the nightingale begins to sing.

Winter is gone, and spring is here,
Now all the baby animals are near.

Katie Morgan (11)
Montbelle Primary School, Kent

HALLOWE'EN

With shadows blacker than gloom,
Witches glide across the moon,
Skeletons rattling in their grave,
All night's dead, trying to be brave,
As vampires hide within,
Their capes whistle in the wind,
A pumpkin on the door,
Drops candy to the floor,
Just inside the local park,
Lies a clearing, deep and dark,
Ghosts dance until dawn,
As if they've never been born,
They prance and dance up and down,
And some acting like a clown,
Children knock on doors to give a fright,
All shout, 'Trick or treat,' well before midnight,
When children are near,
They have no fear,
As the clock strikes nine,
Unfortunately it is home time,
They fall to sleep,
In a metre high heap,
Past has finished acting dead,
And the land lies tucked up in bed,
So goodnight, do not let ghostly bugs bite,
At least not until the next night!

Charlotte Barker (11)
Montbelle Primary School, Kent

GRANNY

We come in, television always on,
Sometime soon she'll be gone,
We walk in the room, her face lights up,
She loves being called upon.

She's old, her seventies' glasses shiny,
Her face is like monkeys' hands,
Time disappearing like sand through a sieve,
This the only way she knows how to live.

Memories she glances at,
Waiting for letters to appear on her mat,
Sometime, sometime she'll, she'll
Be ... gone ...

Roseanne Ashley-Lahiff (10)
Montbelle Primary School, Kent

A PRETTY FLOWER

There is a pretty flower on that mountain,
It is nearby a fountain,
That flower is as red as fire,
To get that flower is my desire.

How I'd love to pick that flower,
I would use all my power,
It would look lovely in a vase,
Just like the stars.

That pretty flower is just delightful,
It glows in the stars very brightful,
But only that flower can glow like that,
And finally I pick that flower where it's sat.

Katie Eastwood (10)
Oaklands Primary School, West London

HAWAII

Dolphins dance like angels
through the silvery, shiny sea.
The blue waves shine like crystals
under the red, red sun.
The white sands sparkle
like gold upon the beach shore.
The crabs scuttle
across the hot burning sands.
The palm leaves sway
in the gentle breeze.
The coconuts swing
from side to side.
Dolphins gaze at the maroon sky
and burning sun and click with joy.

Michaela Bishop (10)
Oaklands Primary School, West London

A SUMMER'S WALK

Skipping through the woods I go
Tripping when I stub my toe
The leaves below me are rustling and bustling
The insects around me are hustling and justling
The beetles and ants are all chattering
As the wind blows they all start scattering
On the ground my feet are pattering
In the trees the squirrels are clattering
When I run I'm always laughing
And the sun is always sparkling
The bees and wasps, they buzz away
As I go to the woods and play.

Maddie Sturgess (10)
Oaklands Primary School, West London

THE DRAGON FROM THE BLACK LAGOON

There is a dragon who breathes fire,
To eat vegetables is his desire,
He's always wanted to join a choir,
The dragon from the black lagoon.

He eats a carrot and thinks it divine,
Then washes it down with a glass of wine,
He watches the stars as they shine,
The dragon from the black lagoon.

The dragon likes to sleep all night,
But nightmares often give him a fright,
Then he likes to see daylight,
The dragon from the black lagoon.

One day the dragon will definitely die,
And in the lagoon he will lie,
There was nothing he could do, but he'll always try,
The dragon from the black lagoon.

Melanie Fung (9)
Oaklands Primary School, West London

MY MORNING

I woke up in the morning
After a night of snoring
I cleaned my teeth and washed my face
And had a bowl of cornflakes
I combed my hair
I looked very cool
And was ready for a day at Oakland School.

Abbaas Ali Ramzan (10)
Oaklands Primary School, West London

THE SUN

The sun is nice and *bright*.
The sun looks like a red-hot fireball.
In the evening the sun sets behind the mountain.

The golden sun glitters in my garden
In summer the sun comes out.
When the sun comes out
It can roast you.
Sometimes the sun looks like a yellow Frisbee.

Luke Weatherstone (7)
Redburn Primary School, Co Down

SNOW

Jack Frost is out
And the snow is moving about.
Snowflakes are dropping
And rabbits are hopping.

Rabbits are in their holes
And so are all the moles.
The snow is white and very bright
And I go out to play at night.

Corey Burgess (7)
Redburn Primary School, Co Down

THE WIND

The wind is very strong.
It makes twisters, whirlwinds and hurricanes.
It picks up the houses
And throws them across the world.

Patrick Short (8)
Redburn Primary School, Co Down

THE LEAF

I am a leaf and I am dusty red
People lie on me to rest their weary heads.
My stalk is sharp and rather thin.
It's as pointy as a huge hawk's beak, as sharp as a pin.
My back is like a frosty spider's web glittering in the diamond sun
I am as delicious as a hot cross bun.
I sound crunching and scrunching and you can hear me blowing
                                                     in the breeze,
As my leaves are tossed and turned and freeze.
I smell like fresh laundry hanging on a line
It makes me feel like a gentle lady that is so very fine.
I smell like a sweet treat
And not at all like smelly feet.
I feel like a rushing river
On a winter's day, I will make you shiver.
I taste like cream with the softest silk
And I am like freshly bought milk.

Caitlin Simpson (8)
Rhydri Primary School, Caerphilly

LEAVES

I am amongst the jewelled leaves
That fall off colossal trees.
Leaves are falling
All around me,
We are at war with the wind!

I make a whistling sound
As I cut through the wild forest air.
Animals below me
Watch me as I dance,
I sound like a crackling crisp packet!

My movement is like an elephant
On a crystal, circus ball.
I spy my friends as they fall,
Softly as they flow,
All I can see of them is their roller-coaster veins!

To touch me is like running on a gravel path,
I am as brown as a grizzly bear.
My contact to the tree is breaking,
I feel myself sail through the night,
I look like a bright, wishing star!

Elsa Carpenter (10)
Rhydri Primary School, Caerphilly

VOICES

The dew on the grass glistened like a sparkling, frozen spider's web,
As the curled silver light of jewelled droplets gleamed in the dew.

The flowers swayed and danced, the bees gathered the warm nectar
From the blooming, posing rainbow shades.

As the leaves slowly drifted to the floor from the lurching, swaying tree
The creaking of the bark and the crunching leaves talked together.

The sea roared against the rocks on the shore with a gurgling and
                                                            slapping of foam,
Tossing sparkling drifting diamonds swaying back and forth.

The wind blows whispering and rushing clouds whooshing
                                                      through the sky.
The hissing and whistling scatter the leaves on the ground.

May Lewis (8)
Rhydri Primary School, Caerphilly

THE PROTEST OF MOTHER NATURE

Once my slopes were luscious green
All sorts of life forms enriched my scene
My leafy trees, branching out into glistening sun rays
Enticed visitors to admire and gaze.

Now my emerald dress
Has been ripped and turned into a concrete mess
Gone are my delicate flowers, my buzzing bees
The protective canopies, my mighty trees!

Row upon row of houses small
All the same, 'I don't like it!' I call
I cry out to say it's a sin and a crime
To make me polluted with household grime.

Don't you realise what you are doing man?
You're interfering with nature's plan
You're destroying me, all for power and greed
And ignoring my pitiful plead.

I give you gifts of pure, clean air
I give you tranquillity and delicate care
I give you beauty of the wonderful seasons
Then you destroy me for selfish reasons.

Take care and listen to my dramatic cries
My babbling waters and chirping birds in the skies
To greedy voices of man who destroy my beauty
I say, 'Think wisely! I'm given by God, to protect me is your duty!'

Seren Thomas (11)
Rhydri Primary School, Caerphilly

THREE DAY TREK

We started at the bottom of a giant hill,
We went through the rice fields which were very still,
People made us food in the hut where we stayed,
I went to the mats where I slept and laid.

In the morning we carried on walking,
We were always talking,
We passed a school and the children came out,
To see what all the fuss was about.
People in a river washing clothes on a stone,
My mum tried to do it but she always moaned.
We ate some rice and went to sleep on a mat,
In the morning we went on an elephant that was very fat.

The elephants lined up in a queue,
Apart from my mum's which was having a poo,
When I got off, my bum was bumpy,
And when I looked at the elephant his head was lumpy.
Do you want to know how we got to the bottom of the hill?
I'll give you a clue it doesn't have a motor,
But it's something to do with water . . .

Maverick Arabskyj (9)
Rosebank Primary School, Leeds

FOOTBALL

Football, football is so cool,
You can play it at your school.
Shooting, scoring,
Hip, hip hooray.
You have scored
A hat-trick today.

Marcus Colquhoun (10)
Rosebank Primary School, Leeds

GALACTIC VOYAGE

I've been on a voyage in outer space,
I've seen so many aliens having a race.
I've passed planets like Mercury and Venus,
Yet no aliens have ever seen us.
I've passed Earth and Mars,
Passed all the twinkling stars.
I've passed Saturn and Jupiter,
I haven't seen anything stupider.
I've passed Uranus and Neptune,
I'll be on Earth very soon.
Now past Pluto,
Now back I come,
Oh my knees are so numb.

Anisah Iqbal (10)
Rosebank Primary School, Leeds

DOLPHIN

They grace the seas,
All calm and cool,
You'll sometimes see them
Act the fool.
Their fins are pointed,
All shiny and blue,
They swim in the ocean
Just like me and you.
They're friendly by nature,
Both kind and laid back,
Unless you're a shark,
And then they'll attack.

Sarah Blakeborough (9)
Rosebank Primary School, Leeds

FUNKY BEAT

Funky beat in the street,
I love clapping to the beat.
Dancing, prancing in the street,
Do you like the funky beat?

Funky beat in the street,
I love dancing to the beat.
Winding, grinding in the street,
Do you like the funky beat?

Funky beat in the street,
I love singing to the beat.
Twirling, whirling in the street,
Do you like the funky beat?

Stephanie Germaine (10)
Rosebank Primary School, Leeds

BUBBLEGUM

Bubblegum, bubblegum
Chewy and nice;
Better than meals
Like curry and rice;
Raspberry, strawberry
Blackberry too,
I could chew bubblegum
All night through!

Rosie Connelly (11)
Rosebank Primary School, Leeds

THE JOURNEY OF MY LIFE

I jolt out of bed,
Get changed, then eat.
I wear my coat, my shoes,
And with my mum skip to primary school.

I get dragged out of bed,
Stare at my spots in the mirror.
Wear black, eat little,
And walk gloomily to high school.

I wake up at 5am,
Wear a skirt, a blouse and a smart new coat.
Drink coffee, eat toast,
And drive away in a flash new car to a busy lifestyle.

I wake stiffly up out of bed,
Slowly change, slowly eat.
Play cards with my old best friend,
In the old people's home.

Fehmina Nawaz (11)
Rosebank Primary School, Leeds

THE SWEET SHOP

As you walk through the door
An ocean of sweet sickly smells
That make your mouth water
Spearmint, liquorice, lollipops and sherbet.

Look around and you will see
Rows and rows of Carambars,
Some with liquorice, some with sherbet
Others with both.

Look at the counter and there you will see
Some large glass jars of all different sweets,
Cough candies, liquorice
All sorts of round balls of bubblegum.

What will I choose?

Stephanie Cogger (10)
Ryelands Primary School, Hertfordshire

THE SWEET SHOP

There in the distance
Stood a gleaming, glittering sight,
I walked across the road.

There stood a smashing sweet shop;
I stepped in and saw rows and rows,
Jars and jars, shelves and shelves of sweets.

I could taste the chocolate melting in my mouth,
I could hear the sweets' voices saying, 'Eat me, eat me!'
There stood a lovely big liquorice bar staring at me.
Behind the counter was a nice lady who smiled at me.

'We have a special offer today on candy,'
I pulled out of my pocket a 50p,
It shined like shining armour,
I turned around at the flashing light.

I think I'll have a midnight feast tonight
I wanted to buy everything I could see!

'Can I help you?' she said to me.

Lois Savage (10)
Ryelands Primary School, Hertfordshire

THE SWEET SHOP

As the gust of sweets hit my nose,
The colours, the lights,
All the jars,
The chocolate all looking lovely and tasty,
The bouncing light reflected off the jars,
All the bright, bulging wrappers saying, 'Choose me!'
Bags full to the rim,
The thick cream, the boiled sweets,
What one should I choose?
They all look so good!

Above my head was a sign saying, 'Help yourself',
I popped one in my mouth,
I swished it round - lovely!
I swallowed it - delicious!
I've got to have another.

A big light went on - the jar lit up,
That was the sweet for me!
I bought it, I ate it - lovely!
I wish I had another.

Becky Alford (11)
Ryelands Primary School, Hertfordshire

THE SWEET SHOP

I leapt into the large shop round the corner from my house
The smell of candyfloss ran past me.
I ran over to the drinks to find a bubblegum drink.

I turned around and I spotted a big selection of eggs,
But not any old egg, they were Creme Eggs.
I don't think you would need lights because the sparkle of
The chocolate shone like a star.

My belly was rumbling, I found a £10 in my pocket
And my temptation led me to all of the sweets.
I brought a sticky strawberry sweet and a load of chocolate
Melting on my tongue.

The bubblegum ran round my mouth,
I went out the shop with a hop
It had a smell that lasts for ever and ever.

Kerry Matthews (11)
Ryelands Primary School, Hertfordshire

THE SWEET SHOP

I can see a display of teddy bears
In glittering glass, transparent jars
My mouth is non-stop watering
Also a liquorice bootlace jar standing
Just waiting there to be opened
Some creamy chocolate smell is in the air.
Wonka nerds in their tiny boxes for only 30p
Some sugary candyfloss in bags for £1
Or on a stick for only 60p
Some fizzy cola bottles that make your mouth go sour
Or a Wonka Exploder or a mini chocolate so soft and tender
I could eat them all
A big chewy strawberry for 10p only
I could buy some penny sweets
But I can't choose but I wonder what sweet to have

If I had it my way I would have them all.

Ashton Fendick (10)
Ryelands Primary School, Hertfordshire

THE SWEET SHOP

When I opened the door,
In front of me,
The glittering wrappers and jars,
My mouth watered constantly.

You could feel the smell up your nose,
You could taste the sweets in your mouth,
Wherever you went there would be sweets,
You felt like you could take one,
You could hear people eating them,
And saying how fabulous they all were.

I felt like I could buy the whole lot,
I could feel the chocolate melting in my mouth,
You could see the light shining on the glass
Like a reflection in a mirror.

The rows of people in the sweet shop,
People buying loads of sweets and chocolate,
The Creme Egg fell for me,
You could see people with their money,
And I had just £20 to spend.
Gladly I went home with something
Because my mum was there with me
I was allowed £2 worth of sweets.

Michelle Partridge (11)
Ryelands Primary School, Hertfordshire

SWEET SHOP

As I walked into the mouth-watering sweet shop
The light on the jars was like a reflection in a mirror
It caught my eye so quickly
I did not see what sweets were in there.

The smell of salt and vinegar went up my nose
The cold feeling of ice cream gave me the goosebumps
There were rows and rows of chocolate bars and crisps
They had everything that you could think of
Unluckily I only had £1.

Lee Wilson (10)
Ryelands Primary School, Hertfordshire

School

At 9am every morning,
Just as the day is dawning,
All the children are out at play,
Till the whistle blows to start the day.
Register, reading, writing too,
These are the things we have to do,
Take it in and write it down,
Black pen only, no use for brown.
Lunchtime comes at such a pace,
Meet in the playground to play chase.
Then it's time to go and eat,
School dinners, packed lunches are such a treat.
The whistle blows again once more,
We all run through the classroom door.
History, geography, what will it be?
We will just have to wait and see.
Books and pens all neat and tidy
Put safely away cos it's Friday.
All the parents at the school gate,
Praying and hoping their kids won't be late.

Emma Johnson (10) & Lauren Irons (9)
Ryelands Primary School, Hertfordshire

AS I GET OLDER

When I was a baby
All I did was cry
Soon I'll get older
And wear a bright red tie.
Now I am a toddler
All I do is play
I run around the coffee table
Chasing my dog May's ball.
Wetting my nappies
Making my mummy sigh
She's very tired
And seems she wants to die.
Now I go to school
No more baby games
I sit in the classroom
And do as teacher says.
Now I'm in the juniors
No more time to play
All I do is work all day.
Now I'm in secondary
Talking not allowed
Doing our homework
Or detention - now!
Now I'm in the sixth form
Wearing what I like
Talking and talking
Until home time arrives.
Now I'm getting married
Nervous as can be
To a handsome man
As you see.
Now I'm thirty-one
Third child has come,
It's a boy... who sucks his thumb.

Now I'm old
Sitting in my rocking chair
Knocking and rocking
Until the night is there.
Family crying
'Cause I'm dead
Ninety-two years gone by
It's time to say goodbye.

Zoe Constantinides (10)
Ryelands Primary School, Hertfordshire

THE SWEET SHOP

Could you imagine - just like a dream?
The blackest Blackjacks,
And the pinkest candyfloss,
The tallest mountain of ice cream.

Look at the cough sweets lying there like
My dad on weekends,
I can just feel it now - the Wonka bar snap,
Crackling in my mouth.
Why do you stop there?
I can smell cakes and
Really strong gum.
All I can hear is the Slush Puppy machine,
And the photocopier that they lend out for £1.50,
And the till opening and shutting every five minutes,
It really gets on my nerves - *ting tingling*.
But let's go back to the sweets,
The flashing lights all around
I want to buy everything I can see
I only have 50p.

Natasha Ince (10)
Ryelands Primary School, Hertfordshire

THE SWEET SHOP

As I opened the door of the mouth-watering shop
This smell caught my nose -
Of salt and vinegar crisps and
Tons and tons of Mars bars.

I saw the chocolate factory
This jar sparkled like the stars and that jar of sweets
Made my mouth water like the river flows
I asked if I could have some and he said, 'Of course.'

And after I bought those sweets
I saw eight bars of Crunchies and
These mouth-watering bottles of Coca-Cola
I saw rows and rows and rows of
Creme Eggs and
I wanted to buy them all.

Daniel Burns (10)
Ryelands Primary School, Hertfordshire

THE SWEET SHOP

I could taste the sweets as I walked through the shop.
The shop had a sweet smell all around.
There were jars of sweets and chocolate.
The shop had a fridge full of ice-cold drinks,
Mostly cans of drink.
In front of me there is a lovely crunchy row of sweets.
Rows and stacks of chocolate and jars of toffee,
Pots of sweets and pots of penny sweets.
Boxes of chews, tubs of Pringles, packets of crisps.
A freezer full of ice cream and lollies and ice poles,
And stacks of newspapers.
There were rows and rows of newspapers.

Aaron Moss (10)
Ryelands Primary School, Hertfordshire

THE SWEET SHOP

As I turned the corner
I could see
A shiny, sparkly sweet shop
The coolest one for me

I walked into that sweet shop
Then something caught my eye
A display of Creme Eggs
Piled up to the sky.

In a corner I could see
A whole 28 shelves of
Twix, Snickers, Maltesers and Mars bars
And my mouth started to water.

Dean Cann (10)
Ryelands Primary School, Hertfordshire

THE SWEET SHOP

I could taste the sweets
As I walked through the shop
It smelled as if
I was at a land full of sweets
You could see lots of sweets in jars
There was a big basket
Full of Cadbury's chocolate
And Sherbet Dib Dabs
As I tasted the chocolate
I could feel it melting in my mouth
When I touched the sweets
My legs felt like jelly
I could see row upon row of sweets
There were all different kinds of sweets.

Louise Dedman (10)
Ryelands Primary School, Hertfordshire

LOVE

Love is special,
Love is sweet.
Love tingles the
soles of my feet.

Love is my mum,
Love is my dad.
Loving them makes me glad.

I love my sisters because
I don't have any brothers,
But that's all right 'cause I
don't want any others.

I love my dog,
His name is Sam.
But he's not as cute as I am.

I love Steps,
My favourite is Lisa.
Just like me she likes pizza.

Love is special,
Love is sweet.
I love my family
because they think I'm neat. (Not!)

Jacey Irons (9)
Ryelands Primary School, Hertfordshire

HOPE

Hope is silver,
Hope smells sweet,
Hope tastes fresh,
Hope sounds like a waterfall,
Hope feels like happiness,
Hope lives inside someone.

Emma Irons (9)
Ryelands Primary School, Hertfordshire

LOVE

It smells like red roses,
Love tastes like juicy strawberry,
It sounds like heartbeats,
It feels like romance,
Love lives in an engagement.

Steven Constantinides (10)
Ryelands Primary School, Hertfordshire

WAR

War is grey
and smells of gunpowder.
It tastes of old socks
and it is painful.
It lives in the battlefield.

Ben Tucker (9)
Ryelands Primary School, Hertfordshire

THE SWEET SHOP

It hit me as I opened the door
I almost fell to the floor
The gorgeous smell of sweets went right up my nose
And gave me a warm feeling right down to my toes.

Chocolate - bars, milky and dark, humbugs, butterscotch, Carambars
And fruitful sweets, all in jars of shiny glass
Raisins, candy sticks, lollipops, and ice creams
Mint sweets all weighed on scales of brass.

Row upon row of candyfloss, pots and
Tubs of sugary sweet, and Murray Mints and gum!
Mars bars and Snickers, yum!
I was so excited I forgot the world I was in
For now I was in chocolate land -
Yes! the land of sweets.

Ben Goodliffe (11)
Ryelands Primary School, Hertfordshire

A SONG OF THE SUMMER

The summer days are coming,
Everyone is humming
An S Club 7 song.

It's nine o'clock at night,
It isn't very bright
But everyone's awake.

Instead they're ready to dance,
I think they're in a trance
Because they're going crazy.

Emma Best (10)
Sadberge CE Primary School, Co Durham

THE PARROT

Green, orange, yellow and blue
Purple, red and turquoise too,
All on magnificent display
As the parrot sits on his perch today.

It doesn't sound like this bird squawking
In fact you could mistake it for someone talking!
Imitating children and people too,
Better watch out or he might imitate you!

He's always cheerful, bright and perky
No, he's not a falcon, owl or turkey,
When you're with him you won't feel lonely
He's Mr Parrot - the one and only!

Elizabeth Muller (10)
Sadberge CE Primary School, Co Durham

MY IMAGINATION

My imagination is totally weird,
Just as crazy as a dog that goes moo.
I imagine a UFO will blast me into space.
I imagine a car can talk and take me
To a world of craziness.
I imagine it raining sweets and ice cream
I imagine mountains turning to jelly.
I imagine schools not existing
And work not being invented.
I imagine living animals made out of paper,
I imagine a telephone eating every word
That is spoken into it.
My imagination is very weird.

Clare Eddy (9)
Sadberge CE Primary School, Co Durham

SUNSET

Sunset fun set
you are the bright pet.

When the night is over
you come down from the sky
and make the light so bright.

You are the colours of
the rainbow.
You are like a fire.

When you go down
you leave streaks of pink
and blobs of orange.

The rays of you are like lightning
brightening the place.

Corrine Best (10)
Sadberge CE Primary School, Co Durham

THE FIFTH MAN ON THE MOON

The fifth man on the moon
Was called Sir Edward Cartoon,
He was really a bit mean
But he did fly Apollo Nineteen.

Sir Edward also invented
For the great King Demented.
His inventions were great
Some got birds to mate.

Samuel George Teasdale (10)
Sadberge CE Primary School, Co Durham

SUNSET

The day has passed quickly,
The sun is going down,
And everyone is leaving
The very busy town.

Look at all the colours,
Yellow, orange and red,
All the little babies
Are going off to bed.

The sunset is such
A beautiful sight,
And all the colours
Are oh so bright.

I hope I see it again tomorrow.
If I don't it will be a sorrow.

Robyn Bell (10)
Sadberge CE Primary School, Co Durham

THE SEA

The sea, the sea
Is after me,
And that is why
I flee, I flee.

It's fun, it's fun,
When you run,
Into the sea
When it's sunny.

Richard Berriman (9)
Sadberge CE Primary School, Co Durham

BOOKS

Write, write,
write all night.

Draw, draw,
draw a lot more.

Words, words,
with a lot of verbs.

Pages, pages,
It'll take me ages.

Book, book
take a look.

Spine, spine
it is mine.

Read, read
the word I feed.

Rhyme, rhyme now it's time,
to end my poem and say goodbye.

Rachel Bird (9)
Sadberge CE Primary School, Co Durham

MY BUDGIE

My budgie sits all day on his wooden perch,
One day he got lost and I sent out a search,
But he still goes out in the world
But I know where he is when I put his food bowl out.

Rebecca Swindells (11)
Sadberge CE Primary School, Co Durham

THE RIVER

The river
a long sleek animal
Who runs along on his journey to the sea
Picking up logs
and hurling them back on the bank.
It glimmers and gleams in the sun
As it trickles from the mountain
Then that trickle turns into a river that goes
To the sea.

Matthew Evans (9)
Sadberge CE Primary School, Co Durham

STAR BRIGHT

Star light, star bright,
In the middle of the night,
Stars are bright in the night,
Stars are light and stars might be bright.

Mrs Wright did not like the stars
In the middle of the night,
She got a fright and
Went to get a little bit of
Something to eat.

The sky is blue and the stars
Are white in the night and
Stars are bright.

Maureen Shanahan (8)
St Blane's Primary School, Glasgow

THE ANTS IN FRANCE

The ants in France did a dance,
But they prance about in France,
They took a chance to dance
But they fell apart in France.
The ants dance from France,
Well they took another chance,
But the dance, well it wasn't worth
A chance.

The ant's pants fell down in France
And they did another dance in France,
Went for a prance (again)
The ants took the chance to dance
But they were too busy to do the
Dance in France because they did
Another prance.

Siobhan Adams (7)
St Blane's Primary School, Glasgow

MY COUSIN

My cousin is so pestering,
But he's resting in bed,
I don't want him to bump his head.

He is sometimes funny,
He's got a bunny in the garden shed,
He's got a bit of a sore head.

Oh he's annoying me,
I feel like jumping a tree,
'Well, well,' he said to me,
When I was up that tree.

Ryan McGinley (8)
St Blane's Primary School, Glasgow

Windy Nights

At night I get a fright
But I have a lot of might,
I turn on the light,
So I don't get a fright
And that happens every night.
Sometimes I go for a flight,
Till night turns to light.

Windy nights are frosty,
And foggy you slip
And slither along,
The ground but
You're nowhere to be found.

Jennifer McGuire (8)
St Blane's Primary School, Glasgow

In The Night

In the night
It is dark,
I heard a noise
It was a bark.

There was a spark
In the dark,
It was not a dash,
It was a flash.

I slipped on slush
I heard a crush,
Then I heard a thump,
Then a bump.

Michael Thomson (8)
St Blane's Primary School, Glasgow

THE LIGHT AT NIGHT

In the night you get a fright,
If your light runs out,
Don't worry or scurry,
You don't have to shout.

If you see a shadow, don't worry,
Or hurry underneath your covers,
It could be your brothers
Doing a scary joke.

Jamie Irvine (8)
St Blane's Primary School, Glasgow

MY BUDGIE PERCY

My budgie Percy is mad as can be,
I love him and he loves me.

He feeds out of my hand and flies
Around the room
And when I play the piano,
He tweets to the tune.

He perches on my shoulder
And nibbles at my hair,
He admires his mirror as if there's
Another bird there.

He has a ping pong ball on a bit of lace,
He has lovely green feathers and a
Bright yellow face,
I love my little Percy bird,
He's wacky, he's crazy and
So absurd!

Maria Kelly (10)
St Cuthbert's RC Primary School, Co Durham

WHAT IS CHRISTMAS?

Christmas is coming, it's nearly here,
The season of goodwill and festive cheer.
Everyone wants to help with the decorations,
Christmas is celebrated by every nation.
I ran down the stairs, I couldn't wait,
Today's the day, it's that special date.
Gifts and presents surrounded the tree,
Hopefully most of them there are for me.
I got to the tree in a real mad dash,
I opened my pressies as quick as a flash.

It couldn't be over, I've waited so long,
It doesn't seem right, there's something wrong,
Then I heard the most beautiful thing,
Nuns singing praises to our king,
They made me feel good in a strange sort of way
And then I remembered what's special about this festive day,
A little baby came into my mind,
Someone who would be the saviour of all mankind.
So I thanked God for his kindness and love,
As I knelt down and prayed to our Lord above.

John Jackson (11)
St John Vianney RC Primary School, Merseyside

HOW I FEEL

Like a lonely horse galloping in the pouring rain,
Like a single bird squawking in its cage,
My head aches and spins as I stand and think,
My heart beats like a bomb waiting to explode,
I want to forget about this day, I don't want to feel this way.

Sophie Edgerton (11)
St John Vianney RC Primary School, Merseyside

How I Feel

Like a mouse cornered in a palace,
Petrified.
Like a snake slithering through the jungle,
Slyly.
Like an eel swimming through the depths of the sea,
Darkly.
Like a dog trudging through the field,
Dully.
My legs are quivering badly and . . .
My toes are shivering with cold,
It was my first day at school, today,
I want today to go, I want to make time tick so . . .
I can go home!

Chloë-Anne Topping (10)
St John Vianney RC Primary School, Merseyside

The Wind

I can blow over a car with my furious power,
I can blow a candle without being seen,
Or blow over people and sink big ships,
I can blow paper away and smash
Windows on giant skyscrapers and
After a day of blowing, I sneak
On the top of Brooklyn Bridge
And go to sleep for the day.

Mark Smith (11)
St John Vianney RC Primary School, Merseyside

WIND

The wind is like a lion
Roaring at the door,
The wind is like a snake
Hissing by the window.
The wind is sweet on a
Summer's day or on a
Winter's day,
It can freeze me inside.

Rachael Scriven (10)
St John Vianney RC Primary School, Merseyside

THE WIND

I'm tougher than the toughest man,
I'm louder than a crushing can.
I'm colder than a piece of ice,
I can make a twister at 5.00 precise.
I'm a white swift flame,
I could go and you wouldn't know I had been.

Michael Roughley (10)
St John Vianney RC Primary School, Merseyside

THE WIND

The wind is wild,
The wind is whistling,
The wind is faster than lightning,
The wind is louder than thunder,
The wind is a soft sort of gentle thing,
The wind is like everything.

Clare Curtis (11)
St John Vianney RC Primary School, Merseyside

I WISH

I wish I was Emile Heskey
So I could score goals every day
It takes me an hour to score one
And that's too bad for me.

I wish I was Emile Heskey
So I could run as fast as a cheetah
But I can just about beat a turtle
And that's too bad for me.

I wish I wasn't Emile Heskey
With all those fans chasing me
And that is so great for me.

Michael Maloney (10)
St Margaret Mary's Junior School, Merseyside

FOOTBALL

Today I'm playing for my football team
I hope the goalie can catch
Because we really need him to,
To help us win the match.

We play upon the old school pitch
Our colour's red and blue
Last time we played against this team
They beat us seven - two.

Now we're playing in our game
I hope that we will win
So that our team manager
Has a nice big, rosy grin.

Toby Sewell (9)
St Patrick's RC Primary School, Nottinghamshire

CROCODILE

Crocodiles bite,
Crocodiles chew,
Crocodiles snap,
They'll come after you!

Crocodiles' teeth are sharp,
Crocodiles' snouts are long,
Crocodiles' necks are stubby,
Their mouths are the size of King Kong!

Crocodiles bite,
Crocodiles chew,
Crocodiles snap,
They'll come after you!

A crocodile's plan is cunning,
A crocodile's plan is sly,
The speed of catching his prey
Is quicker than the eye!

Crocodiles bite,
Crocodiles chew,
Crocodiles snap,
They'll come after you!
They'll come after you!
If you're not careful . . .

They'll come after you!

Karl Patterson (11)
St Patrick's RC Primary School, Nottinghamshire

GOING ON HOLIDAYS NOW!

G oing on holiday is fun,
O ff to the beach we go.
I n our swimming suits,
N ow let's build a sand castle,
'G o and play everybody.'

O ur feet are covered in sand,
N ow we will swim in the sea.

H ave a hat for hot days,
O h! Let's fly a kite,
L ook at the floating seaweed,
'I want a drink.'
'D on't run off . . .
A nd go get some shells.'
'Y ou can have an ice cream.'
'S orry, we have to go home.'

N ow let's all get in the car.
'O h, hurry up everybody!'
W e will come back next summer.

Jacob Murphy (9)
St Patrick's RC Primary School, Nottinghamshire

MY BROTHER!

My brother's eyes are demon red,
His teeth could bite through a solid steel bed,
His fingernails are like menacing claws
And his speeches sound like rusty saws!

My brother's singing is a definite fright,
His snoring could smash a bedside light,
His radar ears are triangular shaped
And his mouth should be covered up with tape!

Daniel Withers (11)
St Patrick's RC Primary School, Nottinghamshire

FUN IN THE SUN

I'm really excited, Mum's packing the cases,
We're going to fly to some far away places,
The plane takes off tomorrow at four,
I can't wait to get through that terminal door.

I got on the plane and ate all my food and
That's when I got in the holiday mood,
I swam around in the pool all day and
Had lots of fun in a holiday way.

The sky is blue as blue as the sea and
The sun is shining as bright as could be,
I'll go to the beach with my bucket and spade,
Oh how big and strong was that sand castle we made.

Now back to school to see all my friends,
It's always sad when a holiday ends.
I'm looking forward to going next year,
To laugh and play and shout and cheer.

Stephanie Sewell (9)
St Patrick's RC Primary School, Nottinghamshire

SLEEP

When it is my bedtime
I want to stay awake,
I eat stuff in the kitchen
And I get a tummy ache.
I hide behind the sofa,
Eating all the sweets,
I keep watching all the programmes,
Even Coronation Street.
When my mum does find me,
Eating all the food,
She goes in a rage (a terrible sight)
And into one of her moods.
She tells me to go back to sleep
And go in to my bed,
But I do not go to sleep (you know)
I stay awake instead.

When I wake up in the morning,
I want to go to bed,
I snuggle up inside my sheets
And go back to sleep instead.

Marc Patterson (9)
St Patrick's RC Primary School, Nottinghamshire

BEWARE!

Beware! Beware!
I'm climbing up the stair,
Beware! Beware!
There could be someone there.

Beware! Beware!
Squeak, bash, boom,
Beware! Beware!
It's coming from my room.

Beware! Beware!
There's nobody to scare,
Beware! Beware!
Let's scare her 'Yeah!'

Beware! Beware!
Oh wow it's you,
Beware! Beware!
Roar! Roar!
Boooo!

Anjali Phakey (10)
St Patrick's RC Primary School, Nottinghamshire

GUESS WHO?

Glasses wearer,
Knowledge bearer.

Earring swinger,
Bell ringer.

Mug sipper,
Paper ripper.

Whistle blower,
Art shower.

Hangman player,
Book layer.

Maths beamer,
Disco gleamer.

Rabbit lover,
Board coverer.

Answer: My teacher - Mrs Summers

Marsha Cotter (11)
St Patrick's RC Primary School, Nottinghamshire

WHAT AM I?

As I stalk the skies,
On high,
Little creatures,
Scrabble by,
Screaming and digging,
Afraid of death,
As my evil eyes catch
Their breath,
I swoop and glide
Through the sky,
Getting ready,
To eat
Nearby.

Answer: Eagle

Stephanie Hargreaves (11)
St Patrick's RC Primary School, Nottinghamshire

THE LEGEND OF THE NORFOLK SHUCK

There is a story from Norfolk,
It's the legend of the Norfolk Shuck,
He's as black as coal and he howls and shrieks,
People try to stay away especially when he speaks.

There is a belief that he who sees the beast
On their heels will soon be dead in the fields.

Daniel Brown (9)
St Stephen Churchtown Primary School, Cornwall

THE NORFOLK SHUCK

Have you seen the Norfolk Shuck?
With eyes like a blazing fire,
And a mane as black as coal.
So next time you're in the woods *duck*.

Walking down the lonely tracks
Be careful of the Norfolk Shuck.
Drivers do look out for him.
Whatever you do don't turn your backs.

Death will come to all that see it,
Black dog chomping at their heels.
If it's you he's chasing after,
Time to meet your Holy Spirit.

Lindsey Hodgson
St Stephen Churchtown Primary School, Cornwall

THE LEGEND OF THE NORFOLK SHUCK

People say that a black dog haunts people at night,
Especially in Norfolk up north,
Black as coal, body full of might,
Hurry home, go forth, go forth.

The wildest gales cannot hide its howls,
He'll follow you while you walk down the street,
Alone at night, over the moor it prowls
Then down to the road, it's on the beat.

Motorists swerve as it crosses the road,
Don't look into his eyes, you're supposed to die,
Along the pathways it has strode,
Look into the eyes and up to heaven you will fly.

Laura Manship (9)
St Stephen Churchtown Primary School, Cornwall

THE BALLAD OF THE NORFOLK SHUCK

In Norfolk such a tale is told
Of haunting and bad luck
For travellers who fall upon the path
Of the fearsome Norfolk Shuck.

If you are out one lonely night
And sense something behind
You are better not to turn around
For fear what you might find.

In Norfolk such a tale is told
Of haunting and bad luck
For travellers who fall upon the path
Of the fearsome Norfolk Shuck.

A dog whose coat is black as coal
With a keen and evil eye
Who follows people at their heel
When they're about to die.

In Norfolk such a tale is told
Of haunting and bad luck
For travellers who fall upon the path
Of the fearsome Norfolk Shuck.

Louder than the wildest gales
This creature is said to howl
And over roads and countryside
The Shuck is said to prowl.

Dexter Havenhand (10)
St Stephen Churchtown Primary School, Cornwall

THE NORFOLK SHUCK

In the black of night, when no one is around,
The Norfolk Shuck lurks on the ground,
He is a fearful creature as black as night,
And if you saw him you'd be terrified all right.
He howls and growls louder than the gales,
People have heard his footsteps behind them when
                            alone on the dales,
Drivers have said to swerve to avoid,
Be frightened without a doubt.

If you ever see him you would probably die,
No one knows why,
As the legend has it, if the black dog is at your heels
Your days will be numbered I feel.

Michael Wray (9)
St Stephen Churchtown Primary School, Cornwall

THE WOMAN AND THE MAN

Eyes like glass beads:
Hair is red and fiery.
She was pretty, that's true,
In the dark corner was an
Ugly old man.
Name unknown, eyes
Like 'gone off grapes!'
Weaving straw into hard
Sparkling gold.

John Knock (11)
Salterforth CP School, Lancashire

DELPHINE

The silk haze
The spiral galaxy arriving at dawn,
The calm sea,
Woman's hair flapping in the wind,
As the rocks hide the bottom of the galaxy,
Water skimming across the shore,
Steps so steep and yet so high,
Fishes splashing in the water,
But the mysterious woman still stands there,
Not a move, she makes,
Light shines off the sun like rays of gold
The night is her face,
The rays, light up the pebble covered beach,
Silence everywhere,
Except splashes upon the rocks,
She doesn't seem to be scared of anything,
Still like a statue,
Not a word to be spoken,
The dolphin's daughter watches over the horizon,
Morning is miles away,
Soaring clouds and knitted light,
All part of her creation.

Michael Haydock (10)
Salterforth CP School, Lancashire

THE CHARGE OF THE LIGHT BRIGADE

Light Brigade
Trembling with fear
They waited for the order to charge
Hoping it wouldn't be shouted
Lord Raglan sent a warning order
Guns and cannons were spotted down the valley
Warning order ignored . . .
Charge!
Was shouted
Every horseman charged . . . praying
The bloody field of death awaited
Nearly all were shot down like mown grass
Almost all were killed
The noise . . . deafening
Cannons everywhere!

My mate Tommy . . . shot in the stomach
Me angry.
We charged, slashing Russians with swords.
We took a run up at Russian artillery and broke through:

(In 1854, 600 men known as The Light Brigade attacked Russian defences; barely 50 returned.)

Michael Worden (11)
Salterforth CP School, Lancashire

THE BIG MEAN CAT

A little mouse got scared
Out of his house,
By a big mean cat
That eats a lot of rats.
With big sharp claws
So he can scare
A lot of mice away.
The mice and rats,
Some have hats,
As they make a trap
For that big mean cat.
When he smells
The creamy milk,
He smells the nicest milk
He's ever smelt.
When he takes a lick, *snap!*
A mousetrap.
Clamped onto his tongue
And out came cry,
From the big mean cat
That ran into the living room.
The big mean cat
Was never heard from again.

Grant Armstrong (9)
Salterforth CP School, Lancashire

A Midsummer Night's Dream

Oberon leaning upon his moss-covered throne
while Puck is fluttering over him with the flower in the middle.

Nothing said, not even hinted, just staring, staring at the flower.
The sun shimmering on Puck's glowing emerald body
with his delicate silky wings just managing to keep him up.

The crystals in his pointed ears are sharp and bright.
While his glowing eyes stare delicately at the flower.

Oberon sits there ignoring his conscience
which is telling him muddled-up things,
confusing things, anything or everything,
just to keep his mind off the flower.

A cool summer breeze made the crisp leaves
on Oberon's crown dance.
He ignores:
An evil smug smile emerges.

Carly Locklan (10)
Salterforth CP School, Lancashire

Football Is Great

F   ootball is my best sport,
O   n Fridays I go football training,
O   n Saturday I watch football,
T   he best footballer is Michael Owen,
B   ut Ronaldo is good,
A   ll the time I play football,
L   ast time I played football I won,
L   ast time I watched football my team won.

Shaun O'Brien (8)
Sir Frank Whittle Primary School, Coventry

SCHOOL

Sitting on my chair waiting for the bell
Boring stuff you can tell
Bored stiff, work today
Was just not my own way!

Teacher shouting really loud
As I stare up at the fluffy cloud
Floating past our window
I realise it's time to go!

I grab my coat, shoes and bag
When the teacher began to nag
'No don't you go, stay right here,
Naughty girl, you are Maria!'

As I finally reach home
Mum shouts in a funny tone
'Maria girl, where have you been?'
I open my eyes and realise it must have been a dream!

Claire Kelly (10)
Sir Frank Whittle Primary School, Coventry

SCHOOL

School I love,
Literacy, numeracy and RE,
When I looked out the window I saw a dove,
My best lesson of all is PE.

Okay, now time for a rest,
Then we talked about Rome,
Now get a pencil, time for a test,
Okay, it's finished, time to go home.

Arr, time to leave school,
I walked through the gate,
Oh yeah, I've got to go swimming in the swimming pool,
I better get home, it's very late.

Garion Huggard (8)
Sir Frank Whittle Primary School, Coventry

INSECTS

Creepy crawlies aren't very nice,
I hate insects,
Especially woodlice!

I like butterflies,
They are quite nice,
I love butterflies,
But I hate woodlice.

The bees sting you,
The bees sting me,
Oh how I hate,
The bumblebee.

Ladybirds are quite alright,
But if they are black and yellow,
They are not a nice sight.

Creepy crawlies aren't very nice,
I hate insects,
Especially woodlice!

Bethany Moore (8)
Sir Frank Whittle Primary School, Coventry

OH NO, NOT SCHOOL!

Teachers wear wigs
They have a long nose
Their feet reek especially their toes
The headmaster is even worse
Sometimes I hear him scream and curse,
Last year I was so naughty
The head teacher called me Shorty.

I told my mum, she did not care,
But then again her feet were bare,
So don't blame me if I start a feud,
It's my mum, she gets in a mood.

The first teacher is very round,
The second teacher gets in a mood,
Friday afternoon is my piece of cake,
But think about Monday, oh for goodness sake!

Nikita Hall (8)
Sir Frank Whittle Primary School, Coventry

DOGS!

Creeping all around the house,
Being as quiet as a mouse.
Her ears are pointing up all day,
She waggles her tail in a funny way!

She's got a little wet black nose,
Her small tongue is as red as a rose.
Her belly is round and fat,
And she always likes to chase a cat!

She always likes to eat her food,
Otherwise she'll go in a mood.
Her little eyes will look sad,
And if I still don't feed her, she'll get mad!

Her colour is a lovely brown,
And she's got a cheeky frown.
She likes to bark at the door,
And run around on the slippery floor!

Rebecca Mortimer (11)
Sir Frank Whittle Primary School, Coventry

JAGUAR POEM

Sneaking through the rustling grass
Purring to itself
Licking itself with its sandy tongue
A golden body and sharp eyes

As it swiftly moves to catch its prey
Its glistening teeth are razor-sharp
Its swerving body moves side to side
It eats anything it sees

Its razor-sharp claws
Can slash a board
Its cunning cars
Can catch its prey.

Can you guess what I am?

Jenna Willis (11)
Sir Frank Whittle Primary School, Coventry

PIGS

Pigs can be fat
Pigs can be crazy
But the thing about pigs
Is that they are very lazy.

Pigs are ugly
Pigs are smelly
They roll in the mud
And have a big, big belly.

Pigs have big noses
They are very funny
They go oink, oink,
And have ears like a bunny.

Lots of pigs stink
They are very pink
They have a curly tail
And eat like a whale.

Catherine Berry (8)
Sir Frank Whittle Primary School, Coventry

ZEBRA

Galloping for some grass
Large animals pass
Camouflage of black and white
The lions and tigers fight

Long black tails flying behind
Sometimes they're very kind
Eating every strand of straw
Chewing every apple to the core.

Ellis Brown (10)
Sir Frank Whittle Primary School, Coventry

ANIMAL POEM!

Creeping, crawling through the grass,
Slimed into a chunky mass,
Sneaking slowly through the night,
And slimes himself through a fight.

Its creepy stripes glitter in the sun
While it's hunting for its juicy bun,
The gungy green, slimy skin
Feels like old rusty tins.

He swirls and tangles round a tree
And slithers like the wavy sea,
It grabs people by the legs
By using his special, slimy eggs.

Hayley Barnes (11)
Sir Frank Whittle Primary School, Coventry

THE SNEAKY SNAKE

Slithering slowly through the jungle
As sneaky as a mouse.
It waits patiently
Gazing at its prey.

Pouncing up a tree
It hides and camouflages itself.
He can't wait any longer
He swallowed his prey whole.

Tired but hungry still,
Concentrating at the ground,
Chasing after its prey,
But the sneaky snake didn't succeed.

Kellie Smith (11)
Sir Frank Whittle Primary School, Coventry

DOLPHINS

As they glide through the glittering sea
I wish and wish that could be me
Watch how they jump over the sunrise
And look at their sparkling, glistening eyes.

When their tails sway left to right
I want to jump in and cuddle it tight,
Its skin looks like wet leather
And it feels like rubber and not a soft feather.

They look so cute when they play
I could just sit here and stare day after day.

Natalie Hales (11)
Sir Frank Whittle Primary School, Coventry

FOX

Creeping through the jungle
Looking for his prey
Quiet as a sneaky dog.

Glowing eyes like burning fire,
Big black nose as black as coal,
As strong as a tiger's legs.

Tearing open rabbit skin
With big razor-sharp teeth
With animals fearing for their lives
Trying to keep their distance
From the creature.

Gary Mead (10)
Sir Frank Whittle Primary School, Coventry

ELEPHANT

Herding through the forest trees
Louder than the loudest drum
Heading to the lake for a drink
Knocking down anything in its tracks

The big strong elephant can be seen from anywhere
Using its grey long trunk to suck up the water
The elephant is as big as a van
They all stay in groups in case of enemies

Its enormous grey bulk
Wobbling from side to side
It stamps on every little tree
Doesn't care what it wrecks.

Scott Garner (11)
Sir Frank Whittle Primary School, Coventry

THE DOLPHIN

Swaying gracefully through the sea,
Like a gentle lamb,
It will eat a lot of fish,
But never any ham.

Glistening like wet leather,
Singing a sweet song,
His fins are very short
But his mouth is very long.

At the bottom of the ocean,
That is where it lies,
It is so beautiful
With its glowing, sparkling eyes.

Aimee Goodall (10)
Sir Frank Whittle Primary School, Coventry

ANIMAL POEM

Crawling quietly through the long rustling grass,
Its skin as white as snow,
The dots on it like splodges of ink,
His fangs snarling like a vampire,
Looking for its prey,
It sees a herd of antelope,
It crawls, it runs, it jumps,
On the ground there is lies,
Its family's dinner,
After the antelope,
Blood around its mouth,
They tuck their heads,
And quickly go to sleep.

Phillip McCluskey (11)
Sir Frank Whittle Primary School, Coventry

ANIMAL POEM

Snake
Slithering through the green grass
It waits to be seen
And it feels dry and green

It waits for hours
Hunting for food
Then puts its long, slimy tongue out
And licks up its food.

It twists itself round the tree
And it sits round the branch
At the top, and looks down
So it can't be seen.

Sarah Thompson (10)
Sir Frank Whittle Primary School, Coventry

I THINK MICE ARE RATHER NICE

>Their tails are long,
>Their faces are small,
>They haven't any charms
>At all.

Their ears are pink,
Their teeth are white,
They run about the
House at night.

>They nibble things
>That they shouldn't touch
>And no one seems to
>Like them much.

But I think mice
Are rather nice.

Stephanie Ledbrook
Sir Frank Whittle Primary School, Coventry

WORLD WAR II

Adolph Hitler caused the war,
He ignored the Treaty of Versailles Law.
Children were evacuated,
Houses were made dilapidated.

Jewish people were put in concentration camps
And turned off like lamps,
The Nazi sign caused great fear
And to this day we shed a tear.

Ashleigh Lesley Hayter (11)
Skelmorlie Primary School, Ayrshire

DRUGS

You see children, drugs are bad,
If you don't believe me you can ask your dad.
If you don't believe him, you can ask your mom,
She'll tell you how bad they are.

So children say *no* to drugs,
Drugs are just bad,
They're for mugs,
So don't take drugs.

Some people think drugs are cool,
But if you take them you're a fool,
Don't be stupid, don't be thick,
Don't become a drug addict.

If you take them you'll go mad,
Drugs are bad . . .
OK?

Ross McKenzie (11)
Skelmorlie Primary School, Ayrshire

FOOTBALL

Rangers are the very best,
Kilmarnock, Aberdeen and all the rest,
Kicking and hitting balls on the chest,
Football is the very best.

Goalie looking out for the ball,
Defenders making a big, big wall,
All the rest have far to go,
The other team will score a goal.

Midfielders kick the ball up the pitch,
Strikers get ready to score.
Their defence is very small,
We surely will score a goal.

Neil Goldie (11)
Skelmorlie Primary School, Ayrshire

ANIMALS

All badgers live in sets,
They are not kept as pets.
They all catch food at night
And eat a lot of mites.

Thick skin protects rhinos from wounds,
Biting insects and meat-eating animals,
A rhino's skin is leathery and
Folded to make it like armour.

The walrus has two enemies,
The polar bear and killer whale.
The walrus is a strong opponent and
Can beat the polar bear in fights.
Fiddler crabs live in warm places,
The male crab has one huge claw,
It waves it at the other crabs,
To frighten them away.

Eilidh Wells (11)
Skelmorlie Primary School, Ayrshire

SPELING

Nag, nag, nag ges the teacher,
'Use a dictionarie and corret the mistakes,
Yoo've got a good bran inside that head so use it for goodness sake!'
I hate speling

'Go back to yoor seat and reed yoor poyum over'
I'm told this every day.
'But miss can't I just leave it?'
Is wat I always say.
I hate speling

It's boring having to do these tests,
So wat if I can't spell?
It won't leeve me ending up.
Locked inside a sell.
I hate speling

It anoyee me when I haff to rub out,
Word after word after word.
Why shoold I corect it,
It's absolootly obsurd!
I hate speling

In my dictation,
Their is lots of crosing out,
Wen I ses the mess of my jotter,
It makes me want to shout!
I hate spelings!

Even in maths I haff to spel
It reely reely anoyees me,
After all it's only a triangle,
So why is called an isausoleeze!
I hate speling.

Lisa McMunn (11)
Skelmorlie Primary School, Ayrshire

FOSSIL AND DINOSAURS

Some people think fossils are dumb and dull,
But I think they're just wonderful.
I like every single kind
They're nearly floating in my mind.

From the smallest ammonite
To the biggest trilobite.
One day I'll unearth a dinosaur
And maybe see its giant jaw.

I love them so much
From sauropods to triceratops.
Some were huge and some were small,
Some were short and some were tall.

And if you put amber to your eye
You may see a tiny fly.
Carnivores were being mean,
While herbivores ate their greens.

Some were bigger than your house,
Some were no bigger than a mouse.
Some of them could camouflage,
Some of them just charged.

If they lived now on our planet,
They would cause a lot of panic.
They would crush all the shops
And they would squash our fields and crops.

Now you know that dinosaurs had
Claws instead of paws
And they had sharp, sharp teeth
And they ate lots and lots of meat!

Stephen Kerr (10)
Skelmorlie Primary School, Ayrshire

CHOCOLATE

Some big, some small,
Some with biscuit too.
Some with big tasty swirls,
I like chocolate . . . do you?

Some white, some black,
Some with caramel inside.
Some with little chocolate chips,
Some with cream beside.

Chocolate bars, chocolate milk,
Yummy chocolate things,
If you asked me . . .
Chocolate is the king.

Chocolate eggs for Easter,
Chocolate truffles too,
Chocolate all for me,
Chocolate all for you.

Double chocolate ice cream,
Lovely chocolate bars,
I'm in a lovely chocolate dream,
Mmmmmm . . . chocolate.

Grant Gallacher (11)
Skelmorlie Primary School, Ayrshire

FEELINGS

I am peaceful when in bed
Sleeping silently dreaming dreams.
I am peaceful when I'm sitting
Listening to the lovely music.

I am kind when I help
Tidy my room,
I am kind when I share
All my sweets with friends.

I am shocked when I get
A great surprise,
I am shocked when I find
Out something exciting.

I am sad when someone
Dies and they are my friend,
I am sad when I do
Wrong and get into trouble.

I am happy when I get
To have lots and lots of fun.
I am happy when it's Christmas
And I get lots of presents.

Stacey Little (11)
Skelmorlie Primary School, Ayrshire

SISTERS

You can get 'em big
You can get 'em small
You can get 'em short
You can get 'em tall

Very annoying they can be
Especially when they follow me
To the disco, to the fair
They seem to follow me everywhere

They always giggle
They always scream
They spend most of their life in a dream

When I'm asleep and when I'm awake
I wish they'd leave me alone
For *goodness sake*!

Cory Rogers (10)
Tenbury CE Primary School, Worcestershire

THE SEA

When I went to the sea
The sea, the sea
I saw a mirror and looked at me
When I went to the sea, the sea.

The sea was inky blue
When I went to the sea, the sea
I saw the whales swim through
When I went to the sea, the sea.

The waves crashed up high
When I went to the sea, the sea
The sea was like the sky
When I went to the sea, the sea.

It came in very close
When I went to the sea, the sea
It was like the water in a hose
When I went to the sea, the sea.

Jennifer Gould (10)
Tenbury CE Primary School, Worcestershire

DOGS

Black dogs, white dogs, brown dogs, blue
Terriers, beagles, hounds too.
I took my dog to the wood and I took him through,
He picked up a rotten shoe
And I said naughty you!

All dogs come in shapes and sizes
My dog is one of the wisest.

People take their dogs to shows
To see how much their dog knows.

Dogs can jump, dogs can fly
Well it's best not to lie,
They can't fly!

Ruth Forman (10)
Tenbury CE Primary School, Worcestershire

THE NONSENSE VERSE OF ALICE IN WONDERLAND

Alice fell down the rabbit hole,
And then she met a little mole,
Sorry, I mean she met a rabbit
I think I'm getting into this habit
I keep on saying all the wrong words
Really, it is quite absurd.
Then she noticed a round table
And on it was an ancient tree
Whoops, I mean on it was a large and rusty key
She put it into a little door
But couldn't fit through it once more
She was too big to fit through you see
So she sat and sulked unhappily
I can't remember what happens next
I'm afraid I'll have to close the text.

Morgan Wrighton (11)
Tenbury CE Primary School, Worcestershire

TIGGER

One night around twelve o'clock
I heard a great big smashing knock.
Then I heard a scratching paw,
Scratching, scratching on the door.
I went to see what was going on,
But whatever it was it had suddenly gone.
I head a screeching down the street,
Then Tigger came and pounced on my feet.
It was silly Tigger all along
I thought it was a monster, I was wrong.

Rebecca Jenner (10)
Tenbury CE Primary School, Worcestershire

Exploring A Dark Cave

When I went to go on an adventure
I stopped at a cave,
My mum said, 'Go and explore it,'
Because I wouldn't behave.

I crept into the cave,
It was really, really dark
And colder than a grave,
The darkness eating the bats.

I crept in even further,
There, there lived a scorpion that said 'moo',
I walked into the creeping darkness
And there, there was a dragon both red and blue.

I leapt into his smooth, slimy skin,
There I found a crystal,
He woke up because I dropped a pin
But I shot him with my pistol.

John Blazey (8)
Tenby Junior Community School, Pembrokeshire

Breakfast

I like breakfast best of all
Frosted flakes in a big blue bowl
Filled to the top with the cold white stuff
And left to turn into a bowl of mush
Then I have some fromage frais
This is how I start my day.

Thomas Barnes (8)
The Cathedral School, Essex

SPORT

I like football
Because it is my sport
I am good at kicking
And tackling the other team

I like hockey
Because it is my sport
I like hitting the ball with my stick
And shooting in the goals

I like swimming
Because it is my sport
I am like a fish
You cannot tell the difference

I like cricket
Because it is my sport
I like fielding to catch people out
And being a batsman and making lots of runs

I like athletics
Because it is my sport
I like running round the track and winning the race
And throwing the javelin a long way

I like golf
Because it is my sport
I have got a good swing
And get the ball in the hole

I like sport.

Matthew Ruffell (8)
The Cathedral School, Essex

WINTER

Everything is dull,
Everything is gloomy
The sun is not
Always shining
It sets early
Everyone is indoors early.

Winter snow falls
Winter rain falls
Winter leaves fall
Everything falls.

Birds hibernate
Their activity slowed down
No singing
Not much flying about
Winter has come.

Winter, winter
Who brought you
Into being?
Is it the unknown
Being of the heavens?

Winter you destroy
The vegetation
Your silence is like that
Of the night
Winter, winter talk to me
Winter has finally come.

Chisola Chitambala (7)
The Cathedral School, Essex

MY FEET

My feet are very dirty
It makes my mother mad
Because they look disgraceful
And this makes her very sad.

My feet are very dirty
Because I don't wear socks
I run into the garden
And I clamber on the rocks.

My feet are very dirty
My skin can be quite rough
I do wash them sometimes
But maybe not enough!

My feet are very dirty
I try to keep them clean
But as I have my trainers on
They're hardly ever seen.

Emma White (7)
The Cathedral School, Essex

CINNAMON

My cat has many funny ways
She sits up on my bed
At night-time when I go to sleep
She lays up on my head.

In the morning at break of day
She leaves the house to hunt and play
She catches birds as all cats do
And then she brings them home to you.

And when it's time for her to eat
She twirls herself around my feet
I fill the bowl that's just for her
With biscuits that will make her purr.

Phillip Blood (8)
The Cathedral School, Essex

THE RAINBOW

The rainbow comes out when the sky is blue.
There is something at the end of the rainbow too.
Could it be something really new
Or could it be something really old
Or could it be a unicorn.
What could it be?
Could it be a clicker for your TV?
Does it say fast forward or electrocute me?
There are colours of the rainbow, red, orange, blue.
There are others, but I won't tell you.

Naomi Hammett (7)
The Cathedral School, Essex

THE THING

I can see a funny green thing.
Is it a little green wing?
Or is it a big thing?
Or perhaps it's a wedding ring?
Or maybe it's a huge thing.
Oh, I can see it's a big garden swing!

Elizabeth Stark (7)
The Cathedral School, Essex

MY AUNT

My aunt had a naughty daughter
Whose carelessness broke a saucer
I suppose in the future
She will wreck the furniture
Oh what a naughty daughter!

My aunt had a naughty brother
Whose naughtiness kicked his sister
Which broke her hip
So she could not skip
Oh what a naughty brother!

My aunt had a naughty niece
Who ruined a home-made quiche
Therefore she'll have no tea tonight
Which will serve her right (ha ha)
Oh what a naughty niece!

My aunt had a naughty father
Who went burgling with her mother
Stole gold rings and other things
But said he didn't know a thing
Oh what a naughty father!

My aunt was naughty too
Scared her mother by saying 'boo!'
What a naughty aunt was she
Because she had a naughty family.

Felicity Clarke (8)
The Cathedral School, Essex

I LOVE TO DREAM

I love to dream
about my stream,
along its watery lane
I dance and prance
in victory as I leap
from hedge to hedge.

I sing and ring
about to call
the victory I
won with no
help at all.

My stream keeps
dancing and
singing the way
I sing and dance.

Its coat is made
of silver glitter
butterflies with their
fluttering dance come
to harmony with my
little prance.

As I dream
my stream carries
on with me dancing
around it,

But when I wake up
my hedge is gone
my butterflies are gone
and my stream was gone
and I'll never see it again.

Emma Hammond (10)
The Cathedral School, Essex

THE PARROT

Pretty Polly parrot perched up on our tree
It was on a Sunday morning with all the family.
Daddy called to Mummy, 'There's a parrot up our tree,
If you don't believe me - why don't you come and see?'

We all looked out of the window and sure enough we saw
A beautiful green parrot, it could be a macaw.
I don't think it should have been there
I've never seen it before
I think it must have escaped out of its owner's door.

Our garden's like a jungle, perhaps that's why it came.
Then Daddy tried to catch it but it flew away again.
I do hope that it's safe as Jack Frost has been around.
It should have stayed at home where it would be safe and sound.

Luke Richmond (7)
The Cathedral School, Essex

THE MOON

He wears a white coat like a polar bear
His head is as bald as a rock
His face is as pale as a sheet of paper
His teeth are as white as snow in a blizzard
He eats cheese from his cheese store which never runs out
He sleeps with the glinting stars
He dreams about visitors from Mars
His friends are planets far and wide
But he has no children by his side
He is the moon!

Alexander Fairbairn (8)
The Cathedral School, Essex

THE DENTIST

What I hate about going to the dentist
is the waiting room,
silent until someone comes and shouts your name out

What I hate about going to the dentist
is the weird smell in the room which is horrid
and the chair squeaks as you sit on it.

What I hate about going to the dentist
is the drill that touches your teeth and makes you mouth shake
like a jack hammer on the road.

What I hate about going to the dentist
is the slimy pink liquid
which you have to swallow and spit.

What I like about going to the dentist
is being given a sticker
and watching my brother go next.

Brinsley Peersman (11)
The Cathedral School, Essex

THE BULLY

Big and ugly, hair gelled down.
Stomp around like they own the town.
Give children punches and pull girls' hair bunches.
Pound them down until they hit the ground.
Make children scream and snatch their ice cream.
Big and ugly, hair gelled down,
Stomp around like they own the town.

Abigail Connor (10)
The Cathedral School, Essex

I LOVE

I love butterflies
I love bees
I love everyone more than these
I love friends
I love love
I love Jesus in Heaven above
I love the wind
I love the sun
When the sun smiles at me
It's such fun!

Heidi Booth (7)
The Cathedral School, Essex

THE CHEETAH

The cheetah lives in Africa
He has to hunt to eat.
He's the fastest animal on four legs
The cheetah catches meat.
He has sharp claws
He is a fierce cat
With spotted fur,
But when he runs he's like a blur.

William Haswell (7)
The Cathedral School, Essex

SPLASH AND TWIGGY

Splash is a dolphin
Silky but tame
Jumping through the air
Catches fish with echo location
Very talented too!

Twiggy is a seal
With lots of spots
And lives in Gweek
Swishes its tail sideways
But very fast!

Bethany Hawkings (7)
The Cathedral School, Essex

MY DAD

My dad is funny
My dad is tall
My dad is a doctor
I think he's cool.
My dad is old
My dad has grey hair
And in the morning
I see him bare!

Elizabeth Bell (8)
The Cathedral School, Essex

SNAKES

Snakes slither
Across the ground
But they don't
Make any sound.
Milksnakes are
Red and white.
Beware!
They might bite!

Liam Speed (7)
The Cathedral School, Essex

WHEN WE SLEEP . . .

When you're alone in your bed surrounded by the dark,
Let yourself go to the place where sheep can bark.
In a dream your imagination runs wild,
In this place you can become your inner child . . .

A mad professor or a caring nurse,
An empty bag or an overflowing purse.

Falling raindrops, a lightning strike,
Riding a silk black horse or a fast motorbike.

An escaped prisoner who's a killer on the loose,
Or a fearsome, mad, rampaging moose.

A coat of many colours, floating around,
As quiet as a mouse, making no sound.

It's not what it seems . . .
Because remember this only happens in your dreams.

You could be whatever you please,
A rich man or a beggar on his knees.
Live up to the very best you could ever be,
The dream is yours and for no one else to see.

Dreams can be lovely, special and caring,
It's not something you should be telling or sharing.

But be very wary,
Your dream could be scary,
So, try not to give yourself a fright,
As you rest and wander through the night.

Think happy thoughts all night long,
If that doesn't work, turn your night light back on!

Kimberley Smith (11)
The Cathedral School, Essex

CATALOGUE OF CRAVING

The chewy challenge of treacly toffee
In practically any flavour but coffee,
And the luscious splendour of clotted cream fudge
Are two of the world's greatest treats as I judge.
Yet smooth, irresistible white chocolate squares
Hold a velvety sweetness to whitewash your cares,
And passing through town on my long walk to school,
The rich smell of cookies has caused me to drool.
My absolute favourite one has to be
A 'double white chocolate' especially for me.

Now putting these glorious snacks to one side;
In you, my friend I am pleased to confide . . .
A tempting feast for me must have among its vital features,
Fresh lemon sprinkled lettuce mixed with tender prawny creatures,
Spaghetti bolognaise with cheese would pander to my wish
And queen of puddings, justly named, would be the crowning dish.

David Robinson (11)
The Cathedral School, Essex

UNICORNS

Unique is definitely what we are with our beautiful spiral horn
No man has ever caught one for we move like a silver ribbon
If our blood were drunk that person would live till the stars fell down
Chasing like shadows through the moonlit forest
Over the foggy clearing they thunder all through the night
Racing like silver clouds over the misty moor
No demon can fall upon this creature for it is pure good
Soaring through the midnight sky is what unicorns do best.

Claire Lewis (9)
The Cathedral School, Essex

GREY!

Grey can be so boring and dull
From a school uniform to a battleships hull.

Grey can be so wet and cold
And unfortunately it hurts the old.

Grey can also be trouble in the house
When you find you've got a rat or a mouse.

Grey can be warm and cute
Like koalas, chinchillas and music from a flute.

But best of all the kinds of grey
Is watching the elephants in the wild at play!

Rosie Orgles (10)
The Cathedral School, Essex

POKÉMON PARADISE

If Mum let me I would play,
On my Game Boy all the day.
First I'd catch a Pikachu,
Then I'd see what it could do.
I tried and tried really hard,
To catch a flying Charizard.
In a battle I used Arcanine,
But he was no match for Mr Mime.
When a trainer asked me to fight,
In a battle I used Magnemite.
I've only just caught Butterfree,
But now Mum's calling me for tea.

Patrick Whelpdale (9)
The Cathedral School, Essex

MY TEDDY

I've got a teddy, he's called Big Ted
He always sleeps inside my bed.

His eyes are brown and his ears are white,
I like to hold him very, very tight.

He's a little bit tatty and really quite old,
The same age as me, or so I'm told.

He's really quite tall, roughly four feet three,
And I know he's there to comfort me.

He has got a few holes where my fingers go through,
His stuffing's coming out and his ears are floppy too.

Mummy keeps saying we should put him in the jumble,
But then she knows I'll moan and grumble.

And though this poem is coming to an end
Ted will always be my friend.

Daniel Schultz (8)
The Cathedral School, Essex

MAX

He made me laugh.
He made me cry.
When I was sad
He made me smile.
He was as cheeky as a monkey.
He was as restless as the sea.
He was like a brother.
He was my friend!

Thomas King (9)
The Cathedral School, Essex

OVER A MISTY MOOR

Over a misty moor a desolate lake waited,
A dirty, gloomy, bottomless shade of grey.
A dull, creaky jetty with a windy rope attached.
At the end of this rat bitten rope
An abandoned blue boat drifted sadly.
The ashen moon lit up the scene
Giving off a pale ghostly light.
Like a mirror the surface of the lake
Made the moon silently watch itself.
Silent like the world is dead.
Silent like a black hole swallowing everything up.
Silent like a cold, damp place.
Silent like somewhere where laughter never existed.
Silent like an old, deaf man.
Silence, a safe refuge from noise.
Silent like a lonely moonlit lake.

Emily Hunt (10)
The Cathedral School, Essex

HATTY

The huge hippo Hatty,
Wore clothes that were terribly tatty.
One day she went to the clothes shop,
And decided to buy a skinny top.
When she got back
The top was too slack,
So she took it back the next day.
When she had done,
She went for a run
And never went back till May!

Sian Barnes (11)
The Cathedral School, Essex

THE SUN

It's yellow, hot and very bright
And provides for us our daylight.
It shines up there for us each day
While we have fun and joyful play.
It's not always there, sometimes it hides
Behind the clouds on all sides
Care must be taken in the sun
Don't get carried away having fun.
Cream must be rubbed on your face
And indeed any other place.
Don't forget to wear your shades
Until the sunlight fades.
It's off to bed for everyone
Me, my teacher and the sun.

James Allen (10)
The Cathedral School, Essex

SCHOOL

I have always enjoyed maths,
I know my tables well.
I'm really good at science,
I made a circuit with a bell.
I try hard at geography,
I know the globe like ABC.
History is my favourite,
Cos Henry had six wives.
I really like swimming,
I'm trying hard to dive.
The teachers also all are great,
And they try hard for me.

Charlie Savage (11)
The Cathedral School, Essex

GAMES

Aahh, games.
The part of everybody's lives.
We'll start with all of the common games,
Like jacks, marbles and fives.

So, we begin with cricket,
A unique sport in itself,
The ball, the bat and the wicket,
And unlike football, not a danger to one's self.

It's really quite nerve wracking
Sweating into your pads,
Here comes the ball sailing towards you,
Wham! Your forehead cracks.

Okay, so it didn't go so well
You think lying a bed
In a hospital ward, ward 3 to be exact.
I'm sorry but your nose will heal crooked, the doctor said.

Now we'll move on the swimming
Grab your towel, goggles and kit,
Swimming's great - it's fun
And it washes out those nits!

But don't get too over confident
And try to dive off the top board,
Splash! Suddenly your stomach feels like it's been pierced
By an enormous sword.

Never mind you think,
Lying in the hospital ward,
Games that don't hurt
Is something that you can never afford.

So if you can't find a game that doesn't make you trip or fall
Just don't try looking at all.

Samuel Moody (11)
The Cathedral School, Essex

THE CAT WHO LIVES NEXT DOOR

He pawed at the door
And began to miaow,
He knew I was there,
But I don't know how.

I opened the door,
And in he came,
For a purr and a stroke
Or maybe a game.

He went to the place where he usually sat,
And washed all his whiskers,
- What an elegant cat!

With his tail curled around
He tucked in his paws,
Sleep conquered everything
I know, cos he snores!

Sarah Hardy (10)
The Cathedral School, Essex

MY CAT SPOT

I have a cat whose name is Spot.
His nose is white with a big black dot.
The rest of him is black and white.
He's really quite handsome and very bright.
He knows exactly what to do when my brother
Charles says, 'Spoooot, I'm going to play with you?'
He's off under the bed as fast as he can
And he doesn't come out for beast or man
Until he can see that the coast is clear
And the two-legged monster is nowhere near!

Spot came to us on Hallowe'en!
A witch's familiar could this mean?
His coat is glossy and his eyes bright green,
They glow in the dark with a luminous sheen.
He creeps outside when the moon is bright.
Where does he go in the deep of night?
Off to collect bats, toads and frogs
Or just to play games with the other mogs.
That is his secret, for as night becomes day
He's curled upon my bed dreaming dreams far away.

Angharad Eveleigh (8)
The Cathedral School, Essex

THE CARNIVORE

As I was walking on my way
I saw a duck upon a tray
I ate the duck and chewed its bones
And then I ran away.

As I was climbing up a hill
I saw a rabbit stuffed with dill
I champed the rabbit and gulped the dill
And then I ran away.

As I was skipping along the street
I saw a rat all plump with meat
I gnawed the rat and devoured the meat
And then I ran away.

As I was dashing to the fair
I saw a tempting, juicy hare
I munched the hare and crunched its bones
And then I ran away.

Amelia Wright (8)
The Cathedral School, Essex

THE VIXEN

The vixen watches over her sleeping cubs.
Waiting.
Listening.
Her big, round eyes glisten as she waits.
A sharp bang echoes through the night.
She waits and waits, but her mate never comes.

Helen King (9)
The Cathedral School, Essex

HOMEWORK

Saturday afternoons are always the same
Spent at the tables as if I were lame
It's because of the homework they give at the school
I do it whilst thinking of swimming pools
And then when I've done it, I phone up my friend
She tells me she's done it, or at nearly the end.

Grace Readings (8)
The Cathedral School, Essex

ROBOTS

Bending, twisting, lifting, pushing, twenty-four hours a day.
Cogs and wheels and square type things with whirligigs inside.
Strange noises and weird language comes from its computer brain.
Designing, making and creating, doing the jobs we hate.
They make cars and chocolate Mars, so we can drive and eat!
Next they'll govern and teach to children making life easier for us.
But can this all get out of order and drive the country round the bend?
Will they take over, have we a clue - let's find out!

Now the robots are starting to walk!
They are walking the streets with eyes like a hawk.
Every move we make they examine closely and report them to high authority!
Now they are starting to build their own craft - an oval type thing that can fly pretty fast!
They could be behind you or in front of you, even so you better watch out, the robots are about!
Higher and higher in the hierarchy they go managing banks and the telephone co.
Soon one will be the replacement prince and no humans will be needed to take his place.
Then we decide this is getting too much and a decision is made to take action with force.
The armies of the world are sent to destroy them but they sense this and fight back!
Swarms of them surround the tanks and take away the army men.
But suddenly they begin to emit sounds of malfunction and defeat.
Fizzes and buzzes with a hint of clashes they fall and break their machinery.
All the jobs are at last claimed back and royalty is back on the throne.
All the laws are back to normal and no more fake laws will exist.
No more bending, twisting, lifting, and pushing done by the robots that's for sure!

James Greenwood (11)
The Cathedral School, Essex

SCHOOL

A school is a place where your children learn,
But sometimes they think their teacher is stern,
They sit at the desk waiting to write,
In their heads they want to fight.

At 12 o'clock it is lunchtime,
And all is very fine,
People are sitting on the benches waiting for their dinner,
Outside there is a winner.

Time to go home,
To see your mother,
And carrying your mobile phone.

***Hannah Mochrie (9)**
The Cathedral School, Essex*

DOLPHINS

Dolphins swim in the deep blue sea
They enjoy being free
Dolphins eat fish
But they don't use a dish
As they emerge from the water
They make an enormous splash.

They glide through the water
And jump in the air
Then swim away with a silvery splash
Then come back with a small dash
They have fun with each other
And play all day.

***Abby Wood (8)**
The Cathedral School, Essex*

THE HEDGEHOG

Rustle, bustle, a bundle of leaves,
Has to be careful - darkness deceives,
There are hoots and growls all around,
But he doesn't make a single sound.
Suddenly something moves in front of him,
He curls right up protecting every limb,
The predator inspects the spiny coconut,
But goes too close and gets a greatly painful cut.
He whines angrily in anguish and pain,
And gives a long howl in his sorrowful shame,
When the hedgehog emerges from his spike-studded den,
He calls a proud muffled squeak
Warning no one to upset him again.

Sam Booth (10)
The Cathedral School, Essex

SNOW DAY

The snow slept silently on the silvery shed.
Snow swept the Earth silently and swiftly.
All the snow shimmered around the street.
When I awoke the world was white like a lamb's coat.
I got dressed and ran outside to seek
Snowball fights, sledding and skating.
I found myself in a snowball fight
With Sam down the street.
I went sledding with Dad
And skating with Mum.
At the end of the day
I fell into a satisfied sleep.

Angus Macnaghten (10)
The Cathedral School, Essex

MY MIFFY

Miffy is my cuddly toy
And always fills me with joy,
He is a monkey, very soft
I'd never put him in the loft.

He always has a big smile
And I've had him for a long while,
I like to snuggle up to him
This has made him very thin.

He's made of fur that's brown and cream,
He helps me go to sleep and dream,
My grandma knitted all his clothes
He really looks good in those.

I love him very, very much
He's so special and nice to touch.

Maria Creasey (9)
The Cathedral School, Essex

LOVE DIVINE

Love is passionate,
Loving to your soul
Let it revitalise you with its beating heart.

Love makes you feel like a song of grace,
It cleans my heart,
It gives me peace, strength and courage,
Love is good!

Angus James Hogg Forfar (8)
The Cathedral School, Essex

TIGER

He's not orange or black like a Bengal cat,
His teeth aren't sharp they're rather fat.
His ears don't stand up proud and tall like pyramids,
He isn't striped like a jumper on a kid.
His eyes aren't red with an evil glare,
He won't stop to stand and stare.
His voice isn't loud with a mighty roar,
He doesn't eat creatures by the score.
    So who is it?
My dear old grandad with the whitest of hair,
Whilst out with his mates, was always game for a dare.
He showed no fear but a cheeky grin,
Not a care in the world for the trouble he'd get in.
They nicknamed him 'Tiger' for his devilish ways,
The name got stuck and was hard to erase.
He's the king of our jungle,
Though the name still fits,
He's the friendliest Tiger and we love him to bits.

Cian Cottee (10)
The Cathedral School, Essex

A POEM ABOUT BACK PAIN

Back pain tortures but it does not kill
It can make people very ill
There's people laying in hospital beds
Feeling sad and holding Ted's.

Joints are stiff and muscles ache
Bottles of painkillers you might take
It's hard to bend and hard to walk
It's hard to sit and even talk.

Try to stretch the pain will ease
Otherwise your body might freeze
Pace yourself and take some breaks
Takes your mind off pains and aches.

Ben Brunning (8)
The Cathedral School, Essex

THE TRIATHLON

On your marks . . . get set . . . *go*
What was it I was told - arm straight or arm bent?
The leg, well it's doing its stuff, leg straight and kick, kick, kick
Off I went
Last two . . . sprint, sprint, sprint.

Out I get for the first transition
Will it tell the final position?

On my racer . . . feet on the pedals . . . *go*
How many laps done?
Lap after lap, legs going round, faster, faster, faster
By the end the bike weighed a ton
I skidded to a halt.

Out I go for the final transition
Will it tell the final position?

Helmet off . . . last section . . . *go*
I started to run, I'd better accelerate,
I was being caught . . . would I be caught?
Sprint there's the finishing line . . . celebrate

Out I go for the lap of honour
It had told the final position!

Peter Hawkings (9)
The Cathedral School, Essex

Dolphins

Swimming in and out the waves trying to catch their prey,
Their shimmering shadows moving frequently as they dive
Not knowing what is happening all around them,
The outside world just standing still to see this beautiful sight.

The noises they create are for calling groups together,
Or for calling families when they are needed
Sometimes their attitude can be unexpectedly bad, just like humans
But you wouldn't see it because of their beautiful blue,
Coat that covers their body like a piece of wrapping paper.

They survive on fish who are swimming in their direction
Their pointy tail is one of the most noticeable features,
But their eyes are so deep and incredibly pretty
Once a baby is born the father moves on,
But the mother stays to look after her young child.

Elizabeth Greenwood (8)
The Cathedral School, Essex

Fire

Fire, fire burning bright
Sparks glitter in the moonlight.
Heat flickers from the centre
Warmth travelling to the outer.

Fire, fire in the night
Stars twinkle at the sight.
Shadows chase across sky
Crackling logs make sparkles fly.

Guy Schofield (10)
The Cathedral School, Essex

THE SEA

The sea is wavy,
Blue and dirty.
The sea is salty.
The sea crashes like thunder on the sand.

The sea hits the rocks
and makes puddles for crabs and starfish.
The sea looks lonely and seeks a friend.

The sea floods the beach
when the waves come in.
The people move back.
But the sea still can't find a friend.

The sandcastles and sand holes
fill up with water and get pushed over
making some children cry,
and other children get excited
and start splashing about.

When the tide goes back,
the sand is soggy and wet,
leaving seaweed and rubbish behind.

When people go home and it is night
or even in the morning,
the friends of the sea are out to play,
and with their surfboards,
they play catch with the waves.

Danielle Pavitt (9)
The Cathedral School, Essex

My Teddy

My teddy is soft, cuddly and cute
He may one day surprise me and play the flute
Backwards and forwards I run with him
While I go to my best friend Kim.
At the park we have fun
While we play in the sun
While I'm at school Teddy is sad
But when I'm home Teddy is glad
Teddy is a special teddy and he is sweet
He is the best teddy down the street.

Katerina Panteli (8)
The Cathedral School, Essex

Space

Space what a wonder
Reds, blues, yellows, greens
Lots of colours to be seen
Lots of planets and stars
The sun, the moon, and Mars
Lots of wonders about space
And you can join the space race!

Edward De Barr (7)
The Cathedral School, Essex

The Fattest Man

There was a fat man on the Earth
Who was 6,000 miles round his girth
His stomach was painted
His poor wife she fainted
And so the fat man moved to Perth.

The fat man was tempted to fly
But couldn't get into the sky
The crash when he fell
Made plenty to tell
And that's how the man came to die.

Simon Schofield (8)
The Cathedral School, Essex

BIIRDS

Up in the tree tops where the birds sing,
All different colours, one two or three,
Eggs in their best ready to hatch,
Out pops a baby squealing for its mother.

Soon it comes to dinnertime,
For dinner it's a spider's spine,
Then the mother teachers them to fly,
Oh no, it's a good try.

Tessa Mochrie (7)
The Cathedral School, Essex

THE BED MONSTER

There once was a monster under my bed
He was so quiet I thought he was dead.
Until one day my sock went away,
It was missing for a week and a day.

One day I plucked up the courage to have a look
I saw the monster eating a book.
'Oi, monster, stop that now,'
So I gave him a punch, *kerpow!*

Toby Wells (9)
The Cathedral School, Essex

Snow

Shivering and sparkling.
Drifting and dancing.
Fluffy and fantastic.
Cold and cool.
Winter is wonderful.
Beautiful and bright.
Quiet and quick.
Falling flakes,
Pretty and pure.
Smooth and silent.
Soft then slushy.

Nathan Dabbs (7)
Trent Vale CE(CA) Primary School, Staffordshire

Snow

Snow can be lovely,
Exciting and beautiful.
It is like sugar.
It is soft and snugly.
Throwing snowballs is fun.
But then it goes slushy
And the snowmen vanish.

Oliver Hopwood (6)
Trent Vale CE(CA) Primary School, Staffordshire

Snow

Gorgeous and great.
Beautiful and cold.
Soft and spreading,
A carpet of white.

Frosty and clear,
Silent and sugary.
Snow is excellent.
It is smooth
And white.

Kayleigh Roberts (7)
Trent Vale CE(CA) Primary School, Staffordshire

SNOW

Snow is fluffy and shining.
And gorgeous and exciting.
It is soft and floats around.
Snow flutters to the ground.
It is excellent.
It's now slushy and dirty.

Melanie Griffiths (6)
Trent Vale CE(CA) Primary School, Staffordshire

SNOW

Beautiful and fantastic,
Exciting and great.
It is fluffy and then slushy.
Snow falls down fast.
It is very cold and white.
Ice is very slippery,
But throwing snowballs is fun.

Joshua Pedley (6)
Trent Vale CE(CA) Primary School, Staffordshire

SNOW

Winter is coming,
It has arrived.
Snow is falling.
It is sparkling.
Snowmen are soft
And shivering.
It is bright.
It floats
And is fluffy.
It is pure.
Snow is exciting and excellent.
It's smooth.
It's frosty.
It dances down.

Jake Thomas (6)
Trent Vale CE(CA) Primary School, Staffordshire

SNOW

Snow falls down.
Exciting and excellent.
It sparkles.
Soft and sugary.
White and smooth.
Lovely and clean.
Snowflakes tickle my tongue.
Then it becomes slushy.

Rachel Rowley (6)
Trent Vale CE(CA) Primary School, Staffordshire

SNOW

Snow falls during the night.
It reminds me of candyfloss.
And of ice cream.
Winter snow is exciting and sugary.
With grass below.
Snow is like the clouds.
White and fluffy.

Thomas Day (7)
Trent Vale CE(CA) Primary School, Staffordshire

SNOW

Excellent and exciting.
Wonderful and frosty.
Slushy and clean.
Silent and smooth.

Hannah Lynch (6)
Trent Vale CE(CA) Primary School, Staffordshire

TREES

Trees, trees, whistling in the wind.
They look like monsters in the wind.
Trees, trees, your branches look like arms.
Trees, trees, in the moonlight.

Luke Ferguson (11)
Westmont School, Isle Of Wight

GRAVEYARD

Walking through the graveyard,
Walking all alone,
The ground is very hard,
I'm a long way from home.

Suddenly I hear a noise,
It sounds like a laugh,
A laugh of little girls and boys
Playing by the path.

I see a lady
Dressed in white
With a baby
What a fright!

I see a ghost
Over there,
That's the most,
That I can bear.

I feel a shiver,
Down my back,
I'm starting to quiver
I grab my rucksack.

I'm running fast,
I'm near the end,
I've just passed
The slopey bend.

My house is in sight,
I can see it from here,
I look at the light,
And I have no more fear.

Joshua Broomhead (11)
Westmont School, Isle Of Wight

FRIENDS AND ENEMIES

Friends are faithful,
Friends are cool;
They're like you, they don't like school!
Friends are loving,
Friends are caring,
Friends sometimes aren't good at sharing.

Enemies are horrible,
Enemies are bad;
They always, always, make you sad.
Enemies annoy you,
Enemies hurt you,
Enemies hurt by saying things;
Enemies hurt by kicking shins.

Jonathan Reading (11)
Westmont School, Isle Of Wight

SPACE

Space is fun,
I'll go there soon,
I'm going to be an astronaut,
I'll see all sorts of planets,
I might see some aliens too.
I'll have a giant spaceship,
A funny spacesuit too,
I'll bring back an alien,
And be famous and rich,
So all I have to do now,
Is wait until I'm old enough,
Since I'm only six!

Georgia Long (9)
Woodland View Middle School, Norwich

THE MISSION

Going on a mission,
Going to London,
Double-decker buses,
Picking people up.
Speeding past the Dome,
Closed down now.
There's the Prime Minister's house,
And there's Buckingham Palace.
My mission to catch that nasty spy,
Starts now in my special car.
Car chase, car chase, help, help!
Zoooooooom! Zoooooooom!
'Bang, bang!' he shoots,
'Bang, bang!' I shoot.
I press a button, ooooh!
One of my gadgets,
'Whizzzz,' super power,
Lost him.
Spying on each other now,
Ready,
'Bang!'

Paul Barker (10)
Woodland View Middle School, Norwich

ONE DAY WITH MY HORSE

I left the warm and cosy farmhouse
Through the puddles in the yard
Snorting pigs and clucking hens
Noises all around.

In the stable very dark
Horses standing there
Saddle on the horse's back
Waiting for me to climb up high.

Off out into the fields
Very bumpy, trotting there
Holding on the reins
Wind blowing through my hair.

Turn for home
Back we go
Weary and off to bed
Ready to ride another day.

Charlotte Lawrence (9)
Woodland View Middle School, Norwich

ON A SAFARI

Swift monkeys and mighty gorillas
Hissing snakes all in the high African trees.
With lions, tigers and elephants
I see them all when I'm out in my jeep
At night in my tent I hear
Squeaks, squeals, growls and howls.
Without my rope I would be stuck
On wrecked bridges with rivers under me
In the long grass I feel snakes
Slithering over my feet.
There are traps everywhere
Nets, beehives and snake pits with bones in.
Elephants with their long trunks and
Giraffes with their long necks.
When I walk in the deep, dark forest
There is always quicksand behind logs.
But all in all if I wasn't trained and prepared,
                    I would be dead.

Joshua Betts (9)
Woodland View Middle School, Norwich

THE VOYAGE OF THE BUMBLEBEE

I am flying through the air,
And I don't care,
I am humming and buzzing,
Looking for some flowers.
I can smell flowers:
Hollyhocks, foxgloves, roses, daisies.
I want to drink their nectar,
And paddle in their pollen.
I buzz past some children; they scream.
I fly in a huge entrance,
I'm lost.
I find a human, she screams.
So do I.
I fly high, and out.
I'm twizzing about.
I find my way home to the hive.

Anna Watts (9)
Woodland View Middle School, Norwich

SCOTLAND TREK

Trekking across a moor in Scotland,
Listen to the rushing waterfall,
Climbing up a mountain,
Herds of deer running by,
Catching fish for dinner,
Getting into a cosy sleeping bag,
Scotland trekking is the best.

Emily Dixon (9)
Woodland View Middle School, Norwich

A JOURNEY INTO SPACE

Four men went into space,
They landed on the moon.
The journey was a great race,
But ended very soon.
They panicked when they saw
Aliens, aliens.
The spaceship door was jammed,
Three were stuck outside,
Shouting, shouting,
For the fourth to let them in.
The journey was a great disaster.
They didn't go back too soon.
That was the end of
Four men's lifestyle,
Because now
They live on the moon!

Vicki Tate (9)
Woodland View Middle School, Norwich

A HOLIDAY TO THE SOUTH POLE

We are off to see some penguins,
At the cold South Pole.
Hop on the sledge,
And off we go.
On the soft white snow,
Seals lie resting in the snow
We have found the penguins,
At last we're here!

Alex Hopkins (9)
Woodland View Middle School, Norwich

THE VOYAGE

The voyage begins; drifting out to the calm, deep blue sea
Following the damp, brown faded treasure map.
I'm sailing closer and closer to my destination
Treasure Island, the place I will find my fortune.

My limbs are dangling over the edge touching
                                      the cool blue water;
White froth floats on the sea like bubble bath,
Waves dance and bob along with the boat,
Plunging my hand in the icy-cold ocean, I shiver.

Through the blue a sudden silver streak flashes past,
As schools of angelfish fly through the water,
Seagulls soar and cry in the sky,
Dancing dolphins dive through the sapphire sea.

Rachel Wright-Carruthers (10)
Woodland View Middle School, Norwich

JNGLE RIDE

My mission today is a jungle ride
To see the animals before they hide.
I bump along in my rusty jeep
And then I see something and have a peep.
I sit and watch the mighty elephants feed
And see a cheetah at great speed.
What's the noise I hear in the grass?
It's a snake slithering past.
Up in the treetops the monkeys swing
Scampering through the jungle is
                              my kind of thing.

Kel Haywood (9)
Woodland View Middle School, Norwich

HOLIDAY IN SPACE

I went on a tour in space
It was a very special place
It was dark but full of stars
I was in my rocket, there were no cars
I was travelling fast towards the moon
It looked so big, I'll be there soon
I passed lots of planets on my way
And as I waved I said 'Have a nice day'
I saw another astronaut pass me by
He was in such a hurry I wondered why
He turned the corner and headed for Mars
Perhaps he needed some chocolate bars
I landed on the moon with a gentle bump
I opened the door and fell out with a thump
I collected some rocks with my new knife
This must have been the best time of my life.

Rebecca Saunders (10)
Woodland View Middle School, Norwich

A DRIVE THROUGH THE COUNTRY

Beautiful yellow daffodils sway in the long grass.
The wind blows through my silky hair.
My eyes begin to water,
A big hare hops in front of my car.
The wind blows.
The trees sway left and right.
I hear the tyres humming on the road.
It sends me gently to sleep.

Victoria Reeve (10)
Woodland View Middle School, Norwich

BORED!

We're going on our holidays,
We're going to the coast.
It's going to take five hours,
It's the journey I hate most.
Mum's doing all the shouting,
Dad's packing up the car.
I really hate these holidays,
Do we have to go so far?

We're going on our holidays,
Do we have to take my brother?
He really is a nuisance,
Can we swap him for another?
The cases are all bursting,
I think we've packed the cat.
And Mum will soon be yelling,
'Has anyone seen my hat?'

We're going on our holidays,
Are we nearly there?
'Dad, can you turn the car around?
I forgot my teddy bear'
I've eaten all the snacks,
But we've not gone very far.
'I'm feeling really sick Dad,
Can we stop the car?'

We're going on our holidays,
How long is it going to take?
My tummy's started rumbling,
'Mum, can we buy some cake?'
I've tried to read my book,
But it's jiggling up and down.
Can we stop at McDonald's
When we get to the next town?

We're going on our holidays,
Do you think we will arrive?
I'm seriously bored now,
'Dad, can I have a turn to drive?'
I can't wait until it's over,
This journey is my worst fear,
'Cause when we've had this holiday,
We'll go again next year!

Amber Kemp (10)
Woodland View Middle School, Norwich

MY KENYAN SAFARI MISSION

I'm going on a safari mission to Kenya
Trying to find big cats
Travelling around in my jeep,
My safety clothes on
My survival kit in hand
I find a good place to set up tent
I reach for my rifle and set off looking for leopards and lions
I spotted a pride of lions eating their kill
I sat watching for a while amazed at what I saw
Dusk was approaching, I headed back to my tent.

      My safari mission was
               brilliant!

Craig Inman (10)
Woodland View Middle School, Norwich

Sunny Day Drive

It's a sunny day, let's go out,
Where should we go?
I don't know.

Why don't we go to a football match?
It's too loud,
Too big a crowd.

Why don't we go to the zoo?
Too much walking,
And monkeys talking.

Why don't we go for a drive?
Past the fun parks where the children play.
It's a hot and sunny day.

Through the forest, fresh and cool,
Past the villa and the swimming pool.

The ice cream van plays a tune
Let's stop for a Ninety-Nine soon.

Nice and lazy afternoon
Let's do this again soon.

Natalie Steer (10)
Woodland View Middle School, Norwich

On Safari

At night you may hear a peep
But beware the cheetahs may leap
Black and dingy in the midnight moon
You will be off on safari very soon
But it is still better than the English weather.

John Fisher (10)
Woodland View Middle School, Norwich

GOING TO WAR

Our voyage is to England
To protect our Queen.
We have to dodge bombs
And take a bullet for the Queen.
If I have to, that is.
In a boat we came
Swaying up and down
Just slicing through the water
Like a torpedo in the water
Hoping we don't get hit
So we don't have to swim
Using oars and rifles for rowing
So we get there faster
Until the Captain says 'Land ahoy'
Now comes the real test
To get on land alive
We finally made it
For years we served the Queen
Now it's time to go back
Oh no, so here we go again
Swaying up and down
Just slicing through the water
Like a torpedo in the water.

Kieron Blundell (9)
Woodland View Middle School, Norwich

To The Beach

Cold beach like the crinkly leaves
Golden sand like the shiny sun
Seaweed slapping on the rocks
Seagulls perched on the cliffs
Pier stretching out to sea
Shells all different sizes
Children running in the dunes
Having a great time paddling in the sea.

Phillip Fordham (10)
Woodland View Middle School, Norwich

One Snowy Night

Cuddled beside the fire hearth,
Coat, hat, gloves and scarf.
All hung on the radiator to dry,
I felt so cold I could cry.
I've been out all day in the snow,
It got so dark I had to go.

Luke Clements (10)
Woodland View Middle School, Norwich

Can You Hear The Moon?

Can you hear
Silver moon
Fighting like a fierce warrior
To conquer the sun?

Can you hear
Golden, tender sand
Screaming like a lost toddler
As wind carries it away?

Can you hear
Green grass
Moaning as flowers
Force through like an angry teacher?

Can you hear
Tiny mouse
Crying in hunger
Like a newborn baby?

Can you hear, can you?

Elin Mary Williams (10)
Ysgol Gymraeg Ynysgedwyn, Powys

CAN YOU HEAR THE SNOW?

Can you hear
The snow
Shouting helplessly
As it drifts to ground like a feather?

Can you hear
Blue sky
Weeping
At the world below
Like an injured child?

Can you hear
The green grass
Humming tenderly
To the howl of the wind?

Can you hear?

Rebecca Steer (10)
Ysgol Gymraeg Ynysgedwyn, Powys

CAN YOU HEAR THE BOOKS?

Can you hear the books
Chatting to each other,
Competing and screaming to be read?

Can you hear
That voice in your head
Screaming like a nagging grown-up?

Can you hear
Light
Pouring down on us
Revealing everything we do?

Can you hear
The slugs and snails
Screaming at the plants:
'We're going to get you.'?

Can you hear
The grass
Stretching to win like
Olympic athletes?

I can hear, can you?

Catrin Hughes (10)
Ysgol Gymraeg Ynysgedwyn, Powys

CAN YOU HEAR THE STARS?

Can you hear
Diamond stars at night
Sobbing in lonely darkness?

Can you hear
Pure white snow
See-sawing to Earth from grubby clouds?

Can you hear
New love growing
Between two people
Like roots of a tree penetrating through hard earth?

Can you hear
Earthworms gliding
Through soil
Like seagulls diving into the sea?

Can you hear
Silent moon
Alone in darkest sky
Like a sleeping child?

I can hear!

Nia Wyn Hopton (11)
Ysgol Gymraeg Ynysgedwyn, Powys

CAN YOU HEAR THE CLOUDS?

Can you hear
The clouds
Peering down
Admiring silent Earth?

Can you hear
Slow, plodding snail
Screaming with effort
On an uphill struggle?

Can you hear
Summer flowers
Blossoming with glory?

Can you hear
The houses
Chatting secrets to each other?

Can you hear
Sleep
Running away with our
Stolen magical dreams?

Megan Davis (10)
Ysgol Gymraeg Ynysgedwyn, Powys

OUTER SPACE

5, 4, 3, 2, 1,
The journey has only just begun,
Zooming through space in your rocket ship,
Do up your buttons, zip up your zip,
Who knows what we are about to see?
A comet or an alien family?
So fasten your seatbelt, why wait?
Let gravity decide your fate.

When hurtling through outer space
Never try to tie your lace,
Your hand will turn a shade of red,
And soon you'll wish that you were dead,
When pain starts coming to your finger,
That's when it'll start to linger.

Stephen Westlake (9)
Ysgol Trap, Carmarthenshire